Sᴛ HELENA

A Maritime History

Trevor Boult

AMBERLEY

To the 'Saints' of St Helena

First published 2016

Amberley Publishing
The Hill, Stroud,
Gloucestershire, GL5 4EP

www.amberley-books.com

Copyright © Trevor Boult, 2016

The right of Trevor Boult to be identified as the Author
of this work has been asserted in accordance with the
Copyrights, Designs and Patents Act 1988.

ISBN: 978 1 4456 5841 4 (print)
ISBN: 978 1 4456 5842 1 (ebook)

British Library Cataloguing in Publication Data.
A catalogue record for this book is available from the British Library.

Typeset in 10pt on 13pt Celeste.
Typesetting by Amberley Publishing.
Printed in the UK.

Contents

Introduction

Many people who love islands love the journeys to them by sea. They may be adventures in themselves, whether of short or longer duration, and they allow the pleasure of anticipating the destination; the first glimpse, near or far, and seeing it grow in stature and detail. A sea crossing often romantically affirms the destination's status as an island, even if it may be served by aircraft. Inhabitants of islands may hold similar sentiments but, as home and workplace, speedier, more comfortable and efficient communication is also likely to find favour.

In the summer of 2016, more than 500 years after the island's discovery, St Helena was provided with its first airport, the aim of which is to connect it to the wider world with international flights. Some four years earlier, the first-ever ship to actually berth at the island did so at a temporary jetty. Prior to this, any visiting ship needed to anchor off the main settlement of Jamestown. All cargo had to be trans-shipped by special barges to and from the town Wharf. The only pedestrian means on and off the island was a short set of steps that were completely open to the oceanic effects of sea and swell waves. It is anticipated that the creation of the airport and modified facilities for visitors to the island by sea will bring profound changes and opportunities to St Helena.

Acknowledgements

The writing of this book has been inspired by the generosity and kindness of Captain W. Langworthy, Andrew Weir/St Helena Line; the complement of RMS *St Helena*; St Helena Tourist Office, Jamestown, St Helena; the proprietors of Harris's Guest House, Jamestown.

With thanks to my wife Karen in providing computer expertise, proofreading the text and support throughout the creation of the book.

Chapter 1

By Sea to St Helena

In 1977, the remote British island of St Helena in the South Atlantic was first served by a lifeline ship dedicated to the purpose. The Royal Mail Ship *St Helena* became affectionately known as the RMS. In 1990, she was replaced by the first purpose-built vessel for the service. This, the final *St Helena,* embodies romanticism from the era of classic passenger–cargo liners. At a time when fresh consideration was being given to provide the island with an airport, and the irrevocable changes it would bring, the author sailed on the RMS in 2003 as part of the ship's company, to document the working life of this highly individual 'family' ship and aspects of the island community that she currently continues to serve.

*

It is a merchant seaman's maxim that the best view of a ship is often through the back window of a taxi. On this occasion, with the heady prospect of a month of privileged travelling ahead, chance would have been a fine thing to look forward through the taxi's windscreen, deluged by a late October downpour and bejewelled by the fluorescent lights of *St Helena* berthed at the Outer Coaling Pier in Portland Harbour on the south coast of England. Looming overhead, the spot-lit lemon yellow funnel, enlivened by the dramatic emblem of the St Helena Line, emanated a warm welcome that was soon to be realised from first setting foot on the gangway.

Broad smiles on bronzed faces beneath the hoods of hi-glow oilskins revealed Andrew and Adam, the mate and second officer. Their ready welcome was to become a hallmark of the ship's company, the bulk of which are St Helenian.

As if in anticipation, the day of departure dawned in serene autumnal splendour, revealing the broad scope of Portland's former naval harbour. Loading and storing continued apace. Scrutiny of the cargo manifest readily confirmed that here was a ship engaged in vital lifeline services: medical and veterinary supplies; pharmaceuticals; mail; groceries and bread; flour; live rams; frozen meat; educational supplies; used cars and heavy plant; engine accessories; telegraph poles, etc.

On the main hatch lids, the optimistic delineations for volleyball vanished beneath a double tier of containers bearing general and refrigerated cargo. In the forehold 'tween deck, a Labrador and Border Collie puppy gazed upward from their cages at the pallets of goods descending from the mysterious square of blue sky. By the wooden afterdeck, the forlornly empty and netted-over swimming pool gaped at the slings of stores disappearing down the deep accesses to compartments far below.

Streaming at the yards, the Royal Mail pennant kept lively company with the Blue Peter 'P' flag; subtle and refreshing signs of both continuing maritime tradition and impending departure. The unhurried embarkation of passengers was welcoming and often personal – the greeting of old friends for whom the ship was very much an extension of their distant island birthplace, and whose staff too are well known, and occasionally close relatives. They were joined by discerning independent travellers, keen to experience something increasingly rare, where the term 'holiday of a lifetime' was to become the blandest of clichés.

On Halloween's night, fourteen years since her launch in Aberdeen, RMS *St Helena* left her berth, witnessed by passengers braced against the chill breeze and hint of rain. A rising half-moon slipped behind scurrying clouds, forewarning of brisk autumn weather in the Channel. On the afterdeck, watchful observers and urgent mobile phone users caught the glimpse of Portland Bill Lighthouse as it pierced the night; the last visual link with Britain for those venturing south at the start of Voyage 60 (south).

As the ship lifted and rolled to the insistent swell, already the homely lights and decor of the sun lounge radiated across the adjacent pale-blue void of the pool, in anticipation of balmy bright days to come. Settled into the cosily cushioned conservatory chairs, drinks in hand, St Helenians who were now resident in England renewed their friendships and welcomed strangers with ready and characteristic warmth.

Edith, aunt of the second officer, was returning 'home' on her three-yearly visits; anxious to return to his 'pre-zimmer days', Donald, absent for half a century, was keen to show the island to his English-born wife; a five-month-old baby was fast asleep in the mother's arms, while Cilla looked forward to meeting up with her brother at Tenerife, after loading a second-hand bulldozer for his quarrying business on St Helena.

Early rising passengers next morning took tentative first steps outside. Across the vista of steely blue advancing seas, ships hull-down on the uneven horizon and an overtaken bulk carrier rose and fell in ponderous fashion, as all negotiated their crossings of the Bay of Biscay. Rising to the challenge of having fun despite the conditions, deck quoits were flung in an early display of friendly or fanatical competitiveness.

Sharing the same local time with St Helena, the blast of the ship's whistle heralded the passing of each noon, stimulating island residents to quietly imagine the current goings-on within their distant households. Across the address system, second officer Adam broadcast the day's navigational information. Near the lounge, his newly off-watch colleague Drew pinned the navigational advice alongside a colourful chart of the Atlantic Ocean, its vast compass stretching from Greenland to the Antarctic.

A thinly drawn line from southern England towards Cape Town indicated the ship's intended track. Each day, a tiny marker flag was advanced a little further along the line that wordlessly defined another twenty-four hour span on the graphite pencilled silvery highway south. In the vastness of the South Atlantic, Ascension Island, St Helena and Tristan da Cunha shouted out their remoteness from the continents and latter-day shipping lanes.

On the third full day, pleasant changes were remarked upon: 'It was worth the wait'; 'this is more like a cruise!' and 'I was up early and saw the horizon was flat – I liked that!' In support, the pool was being filled, its rising water sloshing and foaming to life again. Like draught pieces on a board, tables, chairs and canopies reoccupied the sun deck. Passengers and crew intermingled in their relaxation and tasks, a pompous-free zone of mutual respect, where work may be seen, heard and admired, and a kindly word exchanged in passing. Roped-off varnish-glistening rails gave off a spirited scent for the players of shuffleboard and readers alike, as the arrival in the Canary Islands on the fifth day was anticipated.

At her berth in Tenerife, the orderly calm of the sea passage was replaced by an interlude of intense activity. The ship's warning flag hoists were augmented by 'A' and 'B', as divers gave the under-hull a clean-off of growth, while extensive economical bunkering from barge and road tanker occupied members of the engineering department. As the twin cranes were coupled, the expected bulldozer, dismantled into liftable parts, began the next stage of its tortuous progress towards its new home.

In ensuing days, with the trade wind certainty of fine weather, and the creative attentions of the ship's staff, the traditions of passenger liners were proffered with enthusiasm and good effect. The sun deck hosted the 'Castle Curry Cup' – a cricket match for the South Atlantic Ashes; a proper barbeque dinner; the pandemonium of the Crossing-the-Line ceremony; and the most poignant of Remembrance Day services, held with a proudly fluttering Red Ensign as potent backdrop. As an officer discreetly cast his poppy into the sea in a private gesture, it would echo the laying of wreaths at the well-kept and substantial war memorial on the Jamestown waterfront at St Helena.

'From this approach it reminds me of Ardnamurchan Point.' The comment comparing the western prospect of Ascension Island with the notable western extremity of mainland Scotland gained acceptance from the few knowing observers, as they looked ahead towards the cloud-enveloped peaks of the island, and the nearer outlook obscured by coursing showers. Coming to anchor in Clarence Bay, off Georgetown, with a lazy rolling motion in the crosswise swell, the eight-hour stop-off was a brief precursor to the more lengthy and substantial activity to come, at the ship's main destination off Jamestown in St Helena. As deck cargo was transferred to awaiting barges, and the two puppies were unceremoniously carried down the accommodation ladder, some fifty passengers embarked from launches. The majority were St Helenians returning home after a spell of work on Ascension or the Falklands; the remainder being onward travellers arrived by RAF flight from Brize Norton.

All passengers were to find their well-appointed cabins ready with homely touches, as the catering and hotel staff prepared to serve what had become a ship occupied to capacity. In the dining saloon, stewardess Lina took her black bow tie from a cupboard to add the finishing touch to the impeccable uniform that heralded the start of duty, and she was joined by her colleagues for the menu briefing from Karl the chef, on the evening's six-course double sitting.

The practised skills of silver service continued to be delivered with deceptive ease, despite a significant pitching of the ship now on her two-day south-easterly passage to St Helena. For crew as well as passengers, the imminence of arrival created a palpable and infectious pleasure. Shore-going attire, long since hidden away, was once more prepared afresh, to run the happy gauntlet of mischievous spray from the busy little launch that was to ply the last few hundred yards to home.

The chief officer made the announcement in mid-afternoon: 'St Helena may be seen about twenty-five miles ahead.' Shortly afterwards, many faces were peering forward.

Contact was made with St Helena Radio. The volume was increased to maximum so that the jovial greetings reached eager ears on the bridge-wings.

'What are the sea conditions at the landing steps?' enquired the captain. An anxious pause finally brought the reply: 'Conditions are very good for landing.' Universal smiles reflected genuine pleasure at this simple, yet significant, declaration – the difference between getting home or not. The arrival of the ship at St Helena was always an occasion. The RMS was so much a part of the island despite generally being far from it. As on every visit, all had been prepared ashore.

In the main thoroughfare of Jamestown – principal settlement of St Helena – the arched doorway to the shipping agents Solomon & Company supported a glazed case displaying a notice: 'RMS *St Helena*, Jamestown Schedule. Arrival time 5.30 p.m., 14 November 2003. Labour take-on time 5.00 p.m.' Beneath it was a long list of persons needed for the cargo operations on the ship, the wharf and the sundry barges, lighters and launches.

Newcastle United football supporter Leslie had locked up his joinery business in town; Lionel had downed tools on a new house-build in the island's interior. Many others had temporarily set aside their main professions to adopt their periodic roles as ship's stevedores. Assembled at the wharf with their co-workers, they evolved into a bantering and colourful spectacle. Each sporting highly individual working clothes, with hard-hats of every hue, they donned buoyancy jackets of equal variety. At the sea-exposed steps, they expertly began to board the workhorse launch *Wideawake* that ranged and tugged at her lines.

Close offshore, among an assortment of small moored fishing boats, the dormant cargo craft were coaxed into life, as their crews were delivered to each in turn. As the motley flotilla turned seaward, the RMS dropped anchor, her arrival proclaimed by a customary prolonged whistle-blast, made on this occasion by Donald, to celebrate his return from forty-nine years of absence. It echoed from the high cliffs that give way to the steep-sided valley in which nestles Jamestown. There, on the waterfront, behind the stout rails of the seawall, an eager gathering of the populous waited expectantly. On the shore-leave tally-board, brass tag number 49 was still swinging on its hook, as its happy owner boarded the little orange-hulled liberty boat, duty done both for a month away and for the day.

Returning launches brought agents, stevedores, a miscellany of officials and crew starting a new tour. In the foyer, transiting government staff gathered, about their feet white canvas bags emblazoned with HM DIPLOMATIC SERVICE. Further mustering saw mothers and children depart in their turn, arousing a hearty cheer and enthusiastic waving from the stevedores caught up in the event as they paused at the bulwark rail. Here, a heavy mat of old mooring rope hung over the ship's side, as protection against the jarring of lighters and offloading cargo.

The huge 'outboard' of an attendant barge roared as it manoeuvred alongside. It bore large, empty weather-bleached wooden crates for luggage and the much vaunted air taxi – a novel mode of transport for those who prefer to avoid boarding a launch. A small box-like gondola, the air taxi is trans-shipped by the main crane, like so much cargo, to the delight of its occupants. They must enjoy or endure the same attention to gain the island.

Two hours of hectic activity saw the RMS essentially cleared of human traffic. The ship that so pulsed with life in her daily round, witness to growing anticipation and climax for her passengers, lay almost thankfully at rest. True to her name, *St Helena* had fulfilled her purpose.

In houses across the island, there would be many a joyous homecoming, after weeks, months and many years. The ship appeared content, serenaded by the creak of a solitary nocturnal insect and the quiet music from the World Service that infused the stillness of the wheelhouse. The deck officers too could luxuriate in nights largely off duty. Limited to twelve-hour cargo operations in the daylight hours, it was yet another endearing aspect of island life, its pace finely adapted to the real human scale and need.

On the morning that the members of St Helena Golf Club at Longwood awoke for the centenary celebration tournament, the first full day of working cargo on the ship was well underway. At 6 a.m., the hatch lids had rumbled open, and the crane drivers had climbed inside the pedestal to reach their elevated controls. When the main hatch squares were clear of block-stowed containers, the freed-up spaces in the 'tween deck, shelf deck and lower hold released their multifarious goods. In-between lifts of cargo, on the waiting barges, line fishing in the unpolluted waters found mackerel, tuna and wahoo eager to bite.

As each loaded craft eased away, quickly replaced by another from the adjacent ranks, it headed shoreward or was towed by launch. Confined beneath the bulky cliffs of Munden's Hill, the narrow wharf lies directly exposed to the open sea. On its restricted apron, a modern, tracked crane extended its lattice jib to plumb the craft moored safely away from the unforgiving quayside. Here, incoming waves spend their last energies, ensuring that any arriving goods have to accept their final censure.

In a single line, hard beneath the cliff, containers were stacked two-high to wait emptying, their contents subject to Customs examination nearby. As a classic open Bedford wagon set off for town loaded with boxes of crisps, the tide of cargo had reversed; back-loading had begun. By mid-afternoon of the third day, a forklift bearing a cage of luggage hinted at the imminent boarding of passengers for the return shuttle-service to Ascension.

In the golden light of evening, a pair of self-absorbed Fairy Terns, impossibly white, performed aerial acrobatics across the dark foliaged trees in the town's formal gardens. At the seafront car park beyond, families, now in quieter mood, enacted another regular aspect of island life – partings.

A freak of wind briefly brought the sound of weighing anchor, and then three, long resounding whistle blasts. The RMS had once more sailed away from her true home but, in only five days' time, she would return.

CHAPTER 2

An Island Discovered

At the time the Portuguese explorer Vasco da Gama discovered a sea route from Europe to the Eastern World by rounding the Cape of Good Hope at the southern extremity of Africa, trade to and from India was already the preserve of the Moorish peoples. They regarded the arrival of the Portuguese in their sphere as an invasion of their commerce. By the intrigues of the Moors, and the perfidy of the Indian Zamorin of Calicut, Portugal became embroiled in war with India. The Portuguese King Emmanuel dispatched a fleet for the eastern seas. Prior to its departure from Lisbon, three other ships had been sent as reinforcement to the Portuguese admiral in India.

Commanded by John de Nova, the fleet defeated that of the Zamorin. Returning from India, the victorious ships discovered a new island on the anniversary of Helena, mother of the Emperor Constantine. The island was duly named St Helena. Da Nova anchored in the lee of the island, opposite a deep valley. A timber chapel was built in this valley that later became the site of the main settlement, Jamestown.

The island was then inhabited by seabirds, sea lions, turtles and occasional seals. The interior was completely forested. With abundant fresh water, mild climate, fertile soil and substantial anchorage, and being on the direct trade wind track of ships sailing from India to Europe, St Helena assumed huge importance in the estimation of its discoverers, as a place where water and shelter might be found on the long haul from Mozambique to the Cape Verde Islands, located off the western bulge of Africa. They also assumed that the island had never before been touched by human imprint.

CHAPTER 3

Inhabiting, Immigration and Invasion

The English explorer and privateer Captain Thomas Cavendish landed for twelve days on St Helena in 1588 during the final stage of his voyage around the world on the ship *Desire*. He discovered that the island had been regularly used by the Portuguese on their voyages to and from the East Indies.

The state of the island is described by the diarist of the voyage:

> We went on shore, where we found an exceeding fair and pleasant valley, wherein diverse handsome buildings and houses were set up; and one particularly which was a church, was tiled and whitened on the outside very fair, and made with a porch ... The valley is the fairest and largest low plot in all the island, and is exceedingly sweet and pleasant, and planted in every place either with fruit or with herbs ... We found in the houses, at our coming, three slaves, who were Negroes, and one who was born in the island of Java, who told us that the [Portuguese] East Indian fleet which were in number five sail were gone from St Helena but twenty days before we came hither ... When the Portuguese touch at the island, they have all things in plenty for their relief, by reason that they suffer none to inhabit there that might eat up all the produce of the island, except some very few sick persons of their company, whom they suspect will not live until they come home; these they leave there to refresh themselves, and take them away the year following, with the other fleet, if they live so long.

The writer also noted an abundance of partridge, pheasant, wild goat and a great store of feral swine.

It was at this time that the English East India Company (EIC) was beginning to establish itself. In 1592, King Philip II of Spain and Portugal warned his fleet to keep clear of St Helena on their return from Goa, in order to avoid the predations of English captains who now lay in wait there.

The next British commander to visit St Helena was Captain Abraham Kendall. His ship, *Royal Merchant*, was fitted out in London for an East India voyage, together with two other vessels that included *Bonaventure*, commanded by Captain James Lancaster. Arriving at the Cape of Good Hope, *Royal Merchant* was obliged to return to England. En route, a crewman

John Segar was set ashore at St Helena. Captain Lancaster proceeded alone to India. After many disasters, he reached St Helena in April 1593. Here, he found Segar diseased in his mind, apparently from fear of never again seeing his homeland. Such was the effect of joy at the prospect of repatriation with his countrymen that, for eight days, he took no rest and reportedly died 'literally for want of sleep'.

This first voyage undertaken to India by English merchants was followed by a second, equally unfortunate venture, after which no further attempt was made until the incorporation of the EIC in 1600, under the auspices of Queen Elizabeth I. The ensuing voyage, with Captain Lancaster in *Dragon* found him take shelter at St Helena to replace a rudder lost during a storm off the Cape of Good Hope. The provender procured on the island gave them renewed vigour and, in 1603, they arrived safe again in England.

Both the Dutch and Spanish used the island as a source of victuals. In addition, sea salt deposited in the hollows of rocks was used in curing the fresh provisions. The Dutch were accused of destroying both stock and the plantations, to distress the Spanish who, in their turn, reciprocated similarly.

It is asserted that the Dutch took possession of St Helena and retained it until 1651 when they established a colony at the Cape of Good Hope, after which the island was abandoned. The EIC settled it in the same year.

A new charter to the EIC was granted by Oliver Cromwell in 1657, giving it the right to fortify and colonise any of its establishments, and to transport settlers, stores and ammunition. Given the potential importance of St Helena as fortress and staging post on the return leg from India, the company prepared to claim the island. Two years later, the EIC took possession of its first settlement – the still uninhabited St Helena. Construction of a fort was begun, and a small town grew in Chapel Valley. This original settlement was subsequently named Jamestown, after King James II. In 1661, a Royal Charter of King Charles II confirmed the EIC's right to possess, fortify and settle St Helena on behalf of the Crown.

Despite attempts to attract settlers to St Helena, colonists came only in relatively small numbers. Supplies of black cattle were obtained from Madagascar. Yams were introduced, and some slaves were brought in to work in plantations. Some victims of the Great Fire of London arrived the year after, in 1667. Each settler was given a parcel of land in freehold, but with it went the responsibility to assist in the maintenance of the fortifications and to act as part of the defending force. Mindful of the spiritual needs of their employers, the EIC began a long sequence of providing Church of England chaplains to the island as well as enhancing its church facilities.

In 1673, a Dutch force captured St Helena, but it was restored several months later by military intervention. At year's end, the second Royal Charter of Charles II was issued. It sought to rectify mistakes highlighted by the Dutch capture and to confirm yet more clearly the island's significance as a fortress and possession of the Crown.

In 1706, two EIC ships that lay at anchor off St Helena were stolen by a new antagonist: France. It anticipated associations and events that still lay a century in the future. In 1804, Emperor Napoleon had plans to capture St Helena. Eight ships and 1,500 men had been organised, but before they sailed, Napoleon altered the destination to the Dutch colony of Surinam in South America.

Cheers to the Huguenots!

The Huguenots were members of the French Protestant Church, a significant minority in an otherwise Catholic France. As the Huguenots gained influence in their traditional strongholds, Catholic hostility grew until, in the rule of Louis XIV, all legal recognition of Protestantism in France was abolished, forcing the Huguenots to convert to Catholicism. Many died for their faith. Many also fled France, relocating in Protestant European nations and English and Dutch colonies overseas.

The recruitment by the Dutch EIC of Huguenot winegrowers is recognised as the basis of South Africa's wine industry. Less publicised, the EIC introduced a similar initiative on St Helena, offering Huguenot refugees employment on an island eminently endowed with favourable climate and fertile soil.

In April 1689, as 'refugees from the Tyranny and Persecutions of France', the Huguenot party boarded the Indiaman *Benjamin* on the River Thames at Gravesend. The ensuing nine-month voyage to St Helena was a tedious one, during which the Huguenots were expected to learn English. Instead of taking the normal South Atlantic sailing route via the Brazil coast, ships for St Helena kept to the African seaboard to reach the island's latitude, thereafter heading west into the Atlantic.

The Huguenot party consisted of the leader, Captain Poirier, his wife and eight children, Samuel DeFountain and nine other French Vineroons. The chaplain aboard *Benjamin,* John Ovington, left the new arrivals settled in the richest part of the island, and they were 'highly sensible of the comfortable abode they enjoy'd in this distant Region ... the Misfortunes of their Lives sweetened by the Kindness they receiv'd from their new Masters'. They were eventually able to advise the island governor, 'we have at length fixed upon the planting of vines and the making of Wine and Brandy'.

However, the experiment ultimately failed. Conjecture as to the causes include the following factors: destructive vermin, the effect on the Frenchmen's morale of the island's poverty, or the 'shiftlessness of its inhabitants'. At this time, St Helena was in a state of constant turmoil, with several governors in a period of four years – the first, Governor Johnston, having been murdered. Captain Poirier found himself governor for eight years from 1697. Because of the unrest, Poirier would not have had time to manage vineyards, such that they never flourished.

CHAPTER 4

The East India Company

It has been stated that without St Helena there would have been no British possessions in the Far East. The island was recognised early on by the English EIC as a vital staging post for its ships – the East Indiamen – on their goods-laden homeward passages from India and the Far East. The company's trade monopoly had been largely instrumental in acquiring the vast territories of British India, made possible by St Helena watering and refreshing its ships since 1603 on the return passages of over 4,000 voyages. This maritime service has been accorded as the finest fleet of merchantmen that ever sailed the seas.

For sailing ships to reach St Helena on outward voyages from England would have required not only great navigational expertise but also endurance, in consequence of the considerable extra distances required, rendering such passages lengthy and tiresome, especially for heavily laden merchantmen.

In 1603, the English EIC, newly incorporated under the auspices of Queen Elizabeth, fitted out four ships for its first merchant venture. These were *Dragon, Hector, Susan* and *Ascension.* Commanded by Captain Lancaster, and piloted by the famous English Arctic explorer John Davis, the enterprise proved successful, the ships returning from India with their holds full.

A storm off the Cape of Good Hope caused the loss of *Dragon*'s rudder, and after a fraught passage, the ship made St Helena, accompanied by *Hector.* The rudder replaced, the vessels refitted, crews returned to health and a plentiful supply of fresh meat secured by hunting feral goats, they resumed passage for England.

Under normal circumstances, only two ships annually made the extended outward passage to St Helena, these being dedicated supply ships. A surviving Shipping List for the year 1829 records that over half of homeward northbound vessels came from India, China or the East Indies, and a quarter from islands in the Indian Ocean. About 10 per cent of the ships originated from the Cape, and six ships from Australia and Tasmania – then Van Diemen's Land. Most of the ships were British, but other flags included the French, Dutch, American, Spanish, Danish, Swedish, Prussian and Russian. There were also warships of the West Africa Squadron, American whalers and three 'scientific' voyages.

The EIC decided to take possession of St Helena after an earlier plan to fortify and colonise a particular small island in the Malay Archipelago was cancelled because of opposition from the Dutch who were dominant in the Far East. In the 1640s, the island assumed additional importance as a strategic point of assembly. The North Atlantic from the bulge of Africa to the English Channel had become dangerous to ships sailing alone, and it had become necessary for the East Indiamen to finish their voyages in company, and preferably accompanied by one or more men-of-war.

In 1649, orders were first issued that all such returning vessels should assemble at St Helena and await armed escorts, petitioned annually by the EIC to convoy their ships home. One such vessel, *Success,* arriving at Jamestown for convoy duty brought supplies for the island as well as more settlers, demonstrating the paternal-like interest the EIC took in the little colony.

In 1652, the Dutch EIC had made a permanent colony at the Cape in Africa, but this was soon proved a mistake as the harbour at Table Bay was often an unsafe anchorage for sailing ships. Many homeward-bound East Indiamen could not make the Cape Colony and had been compelled to call at St Helena for water and other refreshment. The Dutch company embarked on a lengthy search in the South Atlantic for an island that would serve as a more reliable base than that of the Cape. This proved fruitless and led to a decision to seize St Helena from the English, either for their own use or to deny its benefits to their trade rivals.

In December 1672, a Dutch squadron sailed from the Cape to attack St Helena. In this, they were successful, but the island was soon wrested from their possession by dint of fine strategies and gallantry from the men-of-war commanded by Sir Richard Munden and troops of the assault landing led by Captain Richard Keigwin. Both are honoured in the names of island features: Munden's Hill and Keigwin's Point. In 1673, King Charles II granted the EIC a fresh charter that constituted them Lords proprietors of St Helena with all rights of sovereignty, and free and common socage – a form of land tenure.

Following the island's capture by the Dutch and its subsequent recapture, the EIC, in order to ensure sufficient numbers of defenders in the event of further invasion, promptly fitted out two ships, *European* and *John and Alexander.* They are recorded as carrying 110 persons, soldiers and settlers, provisions, stores and a prefabricated wooden house as a storage facility for the company's goods.

To every family that came out on these ships were assigned twenty acres of land and two cows. They were freely provided with seeds, plants, breeding stock, labour and instruction. Free provisions were granted for the first year. Thereafter, they were expected to procure ongoing requirements at the company's stores, at cost price.

At this time, the EIC became disturbed by the increasing number of interlopers. These vessels, mostly English, engaged in unauthorised trade with India in defiance of the company's exclusive rights. Special high rates were charged them for water and refreshment, far higher even than those levied on Portuguese ships or those of the Dutch EIC. By 1691, the interlopers had conjoined into a society. Towards the close of the century, an Act of Parliament was passed recognising them as the new EIC. Rivalry continued between the two companies until they were amalgamated and entitled the 'United Company of Merchants of England trading to the East Indies'.

St Helena was transferred to the combined newly formed company in whose possession it remained until being taken over by the Crown. The last two EIC supply ships for St Helena, which arrived in 1833, are recorded as being *Lowther Castle* and *Bombay.*

The honourable EIC ruled their little colony of St Helena paternally and generously for over 180 years. However, on losing its licence to trade, it no longer needed this costly official outpost and yielded it up to the Crown in 1834. It was a heavy blow, from which – as has been historically observed – this peaceful, happy, flourishing British settlement has never recovered: by Act of Parliament, island rule was transferred to HM's government.

CHAPTER 5

Forlorn Hope on the Brig *Good Hope*

Calling a ship by an optimistic name may well reflect the desires of her owners for a long, safe and prosperous career, and the well-being of her crews. For the brig *Good Hope*, this was to be a forlorn expectation for one of her masters.

Engaged for a voyage to St Helena from Cape Town, *Good Hope* sailed in November 1814 and arrived in the vicinity of the island some seventeen days later. Failing to locate his destination and with all fresh water finally consumed, after four days, the ship's master Captain Loudon set sail for the African coast. By this time, eighteen sheep had died.

In his account to council when eventually making St Helena, Captain Loudon offered explanation:

> I was still in hopes of preserving some and took every means to do so until 12th December, when all the food was expended. During this last period 17 more had died. 64 being the number remaining, with the bullock, we that day killed and salted them for the crew, having neither food nor water for them.
>
> Owing to a very light wind, I did not make the Coast of Guinea until 27 December. So on the following day went with the longboat in search of water. The surf then running very high, one of the boat's crew – a Lascar, volunteered to swim on shore in search of it, but had not landed many minutes before he was taken prisoner by a number of the natives who carried him away in triumph.
>
> Having no water left, I made the best of my way to the River Congo.

Taking on water, he sailed for St Helena.

It is understood that Captain Loudon had repeatedly asked for a good chronometer – vital for accurate navigation – and was evidently required to make-do. This was not the only time an inadequate marine timepiece was to inconvenience the island, or the course of a ship captain's career.

In this case, it was to prove fatal, as Captain Loudon, while on passage back to the Cape, took his own life; a tragic consequence of missing the island that caused the loss of live cargo – 1 bullock and 99 sheep.

CHAPTER 6

A Plucky Little Schooner

St Helena's governor and council had made repeated requests on behalf of the inhabitants for a specially built schooner to transport stores, livestock and grain from the Cape of Africa. The result was the 'first' *St Helena*, an early example of a brigantine-schooner. Launched in 1814 on the Thames, on her maiden voyage to Cape Town and before St Helena's population increased after the arrival of the exiled Napoleon, it was noted that the vessel had insufficient cargo capacity and that her hull form was not entirely suited to the seas in which she was required to work. Nevertheless, the schooner went on to provide valiant service to the island for fifteen years. With a crew of fourteen, she was expected to complete six voyages annually during a working season of less than nine months.

This is an example of an early cargo: 77 tons, consisting of pipes of wine, salt beef, sheep's tails, grain, cable, rum, wine and candles. Throughout the six years Napoleon resided on the island, where the population swelled due to the French entourage and a garrison of guarding troops, the island's schooner additionally carried goods for the former emperor.

An experimental voyage to Angola was made, to test the viability of procuring meat there for the garrison, with instructions to the master to 'ship as many bullocks of age 3–4 years as your vessel can conveniently stow with the necessary fodder for the animals, leaving room for a number of sheep, not exceeding 50 and from 1–3 years old'. This venture was eventually proven uneconomic.

A voyage to Rio de Janeiro in 1818 proved overly eventful. Its purpose was to receive from HM ship *Blossom*: 90 tons of Muscavado Maxo sugar, 30 tons of Bianco inferior, 15 pipes of port wine, and 10 mules (young and broken into draft). *St Helena* was suspected of being a privateer by a Portuguese frigate and was detained, owing to an 'unwarranted conduct of a Portuguese officer'. Prior to the vessel's release, she sustained material damage.

Voyage 19 was to be ill-fated for her master, Captain Atkinson. Homeward from the Cape, he missed the six-mile diameter island, thereby extending the ship's voyage. The investigations of a subsequent court of enquiry upheld that navigation had been sound, the fault attributable to a great change in the chronometer's daily rate that severely compromised the accuracy of daily calculations of position, by indicating increasingly false times.

In 1821, the schooner was dispatched to England for major overhaul. In an earlier survey of the ship's hull, critical parts of her structure were found to be perforated from the attentions of marine boring worms. These included the main- and false-keels, sternpost, rudder and planking adjacent to the keel. The schooner's bottom was also re-coppered.

Captain Atkinson was again to miss the island, causing many livestock to perish. On this occasion, it was considered appropriate that his employment be terminated, after which, command was given to Captain James Fairfax. First officer Benjamin Harrison acted in the interim period. When regular voyages to the Cape resumed, it was not unknown for individuals to be transported there for medical reasons. In 1826, an Act of Parliament authorised the transportation of offenders from the island to New South Wales. As it rarely happened that a vessel bound for that colony touched St Helena, the schooner carried such convicts to the Cape for detention, until opportunity arose to complete the journey on another ship.

The vessel's final voyage for the island of St Helena and the EIC took place in 1830, after which she was sent to England via Sierra Leone. She was attacked by pirates in the Gulf of Guinea, being boarded by a felucca under French colours. Eleven were murdered, including the captain. After plundering and unsuccessful attempts to scuttle and bombardment, the attackers left. Survivors successfully sailed her to Sierra Leone. Repaired by the Navy and with passengers, including invalided officers and men of the West Africa Squadron, responsible for anti-slavery patrols, she was erroneously detained again by a Portuguese frigate and taken to Lisbon.

The inhabitants of St Helena eventually heard the cold fate of their ship from the authorities in England: 'We have sold the Schooner. It is not our intention to replace her.' The island was thereafter obliged to make arrangements with agents in Cape Town for the periodic competitive charter of ships that 'we have no doubt may be effected at a considerable saving compared with the expense incurred by the constant maintenance of the Schooner'.

The ship was twice sold. In coastal trade, she sank in a storm in Plettenberg Bay, South Africa, in 1851. It is thought that no lives were lost.

CHAPTER 7

Napoleon

Following the Battle of Waterloo, in mid-July 1815, Napoleon surrendered to the British on HMS *Bellerophon* off the French Atlantic port of Rochefort. The British government decided to exile Napoleon to the remote island of St Helena.

St Helena lay within the jurisdiction of the Cape of Good Hope station of the British Navy. The station's Commander-in-Chief Sir George Cockburn hoisted his flag on HMS *Northumberland* at Spithead, England, and in convoy with two troopships intended to rendezvous with *Bellerophon* in Plymouth Sound. However, *Bellerophon* had been hurriedly put to sea to avoid the serious threat of a writ of habeas corpus being served, requiring Napoleon to appear in evidence at a trial in London.

Popular interest in Napoleon was intense. The waters about the two ships were crowded with sightseeing boats. Silence prevailed as Napoleon descended to *Northumberland's* barge. Twenty-eight others made up the accompanying French party. On 9 August, the assembled squadron, which also included seven more vessels and a store ship, sailed for St Helena.

Although defeated, Napoleon was still regarded as emperor by his followers. A battle of wills and wits was played out between Napoleon and Sir George Cockburn during the long voyage south: they were equally matched.

Cockburn took his role of custodian seriously: 'You may depend on my taking care of the common disturber', he assured, aware that the British government intended to incarcerate Napoleon for good. Cockburn was evidently concerned to win the psychological duel for intellectual supremacy that made up the critical element in physical control.

Cockburn's methods brought accusations of a lack of fine feelings, chivalry, magnanimity and consideration for the situation of an ex-emperor, but he never lost control, and on no occasion was he reduced to discourtesy or emotion, despite Napoleon posing repeated minor but important problems of personal control. Cockburn ably influenced the conduct of his charge without ever losing his cooperation.

During the first day, Napoleon maintained a polite, sociable façade and seemed reconciled to his fate. At times, however, especially when reminded of his increasing distance from Europe, he became dejected. Adding to these moods was a repressed anger that followed checks on his claims to special treatment. As Cockburn was responsible for these checks, the moods added to difficulties of management, especially in the first week when Napoleon tried to exact from English officers the deference to which he was accustomed.

From this time onwards, relations gradually improved. On 15 August – Napoleon's birthday – Cockburn made him 'compliments upon it and drank his health, which civility he seemed to appreciate'. On the 27th, Cockburn caused the whole squadron to steer between Gomera and Palma in the Canary Islands simply to gratify Napoleon's curiosity.

It is recorded of Frederick Bedwell, Master's Mate, that 'needing exercise, Napoleon used to fence with this young officer. On one occasion the young lieutenant Bedwell lifted a button off the ex-Emperor's jacket. Napoleon graciously handed it to him to keep as a souvenir.'

One factor helping to stabilise relations was the invariable routine into which meetings between French and English fell. The patterns of their respective lives coincided only in the evenings. At dinner, Cockburn always sat beside Napoleon, their places requiring observance of essential courtesies. At table, Cockburn's fluency in French permitted him to communicate at will, his conversations with Napoleon commanding the attention of all diners. Cockburn was able to draw him out, so that Napoleon's reminiscences became the main accompaniment to meals. This was followed by exercise on deck, in which Cockburn and Napoleon usually walked together, mostly out of earshot.

These considerations were regarded as vital to the understanding they developed. Both gave equally: Cockburn flattered by his questions; Napoleon rewarded with his politeness. Finally, evenings were completed by an hour or more of cards.

By studying and humanising him, Napoleon diminished in Cockburn's estimation. In contrast, Cockburn seems to have risen in respect among the French party, especially for his professional competence. On the day when St Helena was sighted, numerous suggestions were made as to when they would see land. It is recorded that Cockburn 'decided we should see it at six o'clock, and so correct was he in his calculations that the time we saw it did not differ a *minute* ... at which Bonaparte and all the French party seemed much astonished.'

In October 1815, HM's sloop *Icarus* brought the astonishing news to St Helena that Napoleon Bonaparte was on his way. He arrived only four days later. Longwood – the former residence of the lieutenant governor of the EIC, who managed St Helena – was given over as the residence of Napoleon, who died there in 1821. In his will, Napoleon stated his wish to be buried on the banks of the Seine in France, but the island's governor insisted the location be on St Helena, in what was then known as the Valley of the Willows.

In 1840, the French frigate *La Belle Poule,* accompanied by the corvette *Favourite,* arrived at St Helena with HRH the Prince de Joinville and his suite, to remove Napoleon's remains to France. With great ceremony, the coffin was exhumed on 15 October, the anniversary of the day when *Northumberland* originally reached the island. A poignant gesture from the inhabitants was the gift of a fine silk flag made by three young St Helenian ladies. It was flown on the boat that tendered Napoleon's remains to *La Belle Poule.* The ship had been painted black for the duration of her unique assignment.

CHAPTER 8

Horseplay

St Helena was to become an unlikely venue for a preoccupation often referred to as the Sport of Kings, which survived for more than a century.

In the island's *Racing Calendar* for 1817, the Maiden Meeting of the St Helena Turf Club was billed as a two-day event, held in April, consisting of eight races: four two-horse matches and four plates, including a handicap and sweepstake. The races were run at Deadwood, and the course has been described as an 'excellent mile-and-a-half'.

It has been asserted that the races had been instituted by the honourable Henry John Rous, styled as the second son of the Earl of Stradbroke. Rous had arrived at St Helena as a lieutenant on HMS *Conqueror* and was soon promoted captain of HMS *Podargus* and then HMS *Mosquito*. During his two-year stay on the island, he attended four race meetings. Still in his early twenties, he dominated the racing scene, by dint of personality, physique and expertise.

Rous was to become a household name in Victorian England, through his formative experiences at his father's stables and on Newmarket Heath. After wartime service at sea, and the coming of peace that brought him to St Helena, the Deadwood Races provided a stamping ground in race management. Soon after his return to England, he was elected to the Jockey Club. Leaving the sea in 1836, he began the career that eventually made him Admiral Rous, 'the dictator of the English Turf'. Yet, in biographies about him, there are evidently no references to his experiences on St Helena. A recollection by a colleague on the island acknowledges how Rous ruled over the St Helena racing 'with all the authority he so long exercised at Newmarket'.

In 1818, the East Indiaman *Lady Carrington* delivered a dray horse to the island for use on the Jamestown Wharf. As a joke, an officer made a wager that he could trot the horse at Deadwood against any 'Island nag'. The ensuing challenge attracted great curiosity that was eventually recorded in the London newspaper *The Courier*:

At the appointed time the gentleman who rode the 'daisy-cutter' was upon the ground waiting for his opponent, the knight of the dray-horse, who soon made his appearance over the top of the last hill on his way from town to Deadwood [...] accoutred with a large white frock coat, a white hat with slouching brim, large top boots and his dexter hand flourishing a long whip.

They started, and bets ran high against poor Dobbin; but his opponent, perhaps scorning such a competitor, [...] soon broke off into his accustomed two up and two down, and was consequently obliged to return and start anew ... The tide now turned in Dobbin's favour, who all this while kept on the even tenor of his trot [...] he came in winner of the race amidst the loud laughter and acclamation of almost the whole population of the island.

As Napoleon's residence at Longwood Old House overlooked the racecourse, he usually watched discreetly through a telescope, although his own horses were never raced. The island's governor presented at least two plates annually, always attending with a large party, rendering the Turf Club meetings major occasions of the St Helena government's commitment to 'corporate entertainment'.

Two horses had come with Napoleon from France: Frengant and Vizir. The Longwood stables contained some sixteen horses, among the finest on the island. Ten were ordered from the Cape for carriage and staff use. Members of the entourage also brought their own and stabled them at Longwood.

The withdrawal of the guarding garrison, following Napoleon's death in 1821, might have also sounded the death knell of the St Helena Turf Club. The subsequent halving of the population, the collapse of its former associated prosperity, the loss of horses, riders and expertise, and the impetus for the sport, all rendered its survival doubtful. Yet, it did survive, but is little recorded.

When the island was transferred to the Crown and the first colonial governor took office in 1836, the EIC's civil and military servants were dismissed. Most were to leave the island and with them went the assets of the natural supporters of the Turf Club. But, yet again it soldiered on. New supporters of the club reportedly came from those who benefited from the change of regime: prosperous merchants of Jamestown and opportunistic civil servants. The swansong of the Deadwood Races is considered the Easter meeting of 1923, with an ambitious programme of seven races.

From the beginning, the Deadwood Races were meant as entertainment, and as such, it was the tradition that endured. Throughout, 'Derby Days at Deadwood' provided a social and cultural spectacle, initially inspired by a naval lieutenant, fortuitously assigned to the St Helena station.

CHAPTER 9

In Matters of Faith

In 1845, the brig *Velox* arrived at St Helena from the Cape of Good Hope. Aboard was a Scottish evangelist, bound for the island. James McGregor Bertram had previously been ministering to guano workers at Saldanha Bay, some sixty miles northwards of Cape Town. Expatriate St Helenians had persuaded him to relieve what they had described as the spiritual desolation of their island home.

St Helena is home to the oldest Anglican Church in the southern hemisphere, admired by Captain Cook. Supremacy by Anglicans had never been successfully challenged since the island was first settled and fortified by the EIC. Dissent was discouraged by its directors who made clear that subversion of the establishment would be viewed gravely. Yet St Helena had been home to many religious doctrines, none of which were a bar to inhabiting the island.

In 1834, St Helena became a Crown colony, ending the EIC's paternalistic rule. In the aftermath of the transfer, social disorder had swelled and drunks even disrupted Sunday worship. The timely arrival of Bertram was a godsend. Bertram addressed audiences that congregated in private houses. Within a fortnight, a management committee consolidated the island-wide coverage by appointing lay preachers, setting up Sunday schools and renting a Mission House in Jamestown.

Despite moves from alarmed Anglicans, Bertram's appeal did not waver. Under the banner of 'The Christian Mission from the Cape of Good Hope to St Helena', financial backing and support was sustained from important individuals and expatriate islanders at the Cape. The master of *Velox,* Captain James Adams, gave Bertram and his family free passages.

Reports that Roman Catholic priests were to serve the new St Helena Regiment persuaded Bertram to believe that dissatisfactions were instrumental in bringing islanders to the fold. The neglected part of the community also felt more at ease in less formal settings than High Church. Bertram had vital support from a wide range of St Helena society, receiving a sympathetic initial welcome from the governor and backing by businessmen.

By 1850, the St Helena Mission was well established, such that Bertram felt he could trust it to thrive under local leadership, freeing him to raise funds overseas. In this, he was successful, but the mission also became known and respected wherever he went. It brought closer links with the wider Baptist movement, and in 1854, their new building opened in Jamestown as the Baptist Mission Church. Bertram retired in 1866, returning to Dumfries in Scotland.

The opening of the Suez Canal in 1869 brought about a considerable reduction in shipping calling at St Helena. Resultant unemployment caused families to leave for the Cape and consequent reduction in Baptist membership. At the close of the nineteenth century, support for the island's Baptists reverted to the Cape.

In March 1849, the first bishop of Cape Town Robert Gray visited St Helena. This was the inaugural visit by an Anglican bishop and thus the first confirmations on the island; a total of 366 individuals.

St Helena remains proud of its British traditions, among which are the origins of its religious heritage – of both the establishment and range of non-conformist communities.

CHAPTER 10

A Magnet for Science

Edmond Halley was a British astronomer and mathematician most commonly known for the comet named after him, following the calculations he made of its orbit. In 1673, Halley entered Queen's College, Oxford. Three years later, following an introduction to the Astronomer Royal John Flamsteed, Halley was encouraged to study astronomy. Inspired by Flamsteed's work of using a telescope to compile an accurate catalogue of northern stars, Halley determined to do similarly for the southern hemisphere.

Backed financially by his father and with support from King Charles II, Halley set sail in 1676 on the East Indiaman *Unity* for St Helena, the southernmost British territory in the South Atlantic. Although not a perfect location for celestial observations, often frustrated by unhelpful weather, Halley spent a year and a half cataloguing 341 southern hemisphere stars, discovered a star cluster, observed a transit of Mercury across the sun, and found that some stars had become fainter since their observation in antiquity. The observatory he set up was the first of five such facilities on St Helena.

Halley returned to England and published his star catalogue in 1678. It was the first such work containing locations of southern stars determined by telescope, and it established his reputation as an astronomer. In the same year, he was elected a fellow of the Royal Society – at twenty-two, its youngest member. Although he had left Oxford without a degree, he was soon regarded as one of the prominent astronomers of the day and, with the intercession of the king, was conferred an MA from the University of Oxford.

Halley's observations of Mercury's transit, from St Helena, excited him about the potential of such occurrences that he urged the Royal Society to track the next transit of Venus, which, like the return of Halley's Comet, he could not possibly live long enough to see for himself. He argued convincingly that many careful observations of the transit, taken from widely separated points on the globe, would reveal the distance between Earth and the sun. It was a suggestion to be acted on over forty years later, and which again featured St Helena.

Halley briefly revisited the island in 1700 while returning to England on a voyage of scientific discovery. Desirous of better magnetic charts of the Atlantic, the British Admiralty enabled Halley to conduct magnetic surveys, providing him with a vessel – *Paramour* – considered to be the first built expressly as a research ship for the Royal Navy, and this the first sea voyage undertaken for purely scientific endeavour. By February 1700, in an effort to discover the anticipated land of terra incognita, *Paramour* had reached as far south as the Antarctic Convergence, the boundary between the water masses of the Atlantic and Antarctica.

Edmond Halley was the first of many scientists to carry out researches on St Helena. Later, a notable astronomer – Nevil Maskelyne – was instrumental in realising Halley's recommendation to use St Helena as an invaluable base for further particular observations. Remembered by history as 'the seaman's astronomer', Maskelyne's submission to the Royal Society made due acknowledgement to Halley's idea: 'which phenomenon was first proposed by the late excellent Dr Halley ... as a proper means of determining the sun's parallax [an indicator of distance] to a great degree of exactness.' In connection with Sirius, the brightest star in the heavens, Maskelyne further advised: 'at the island of St Helena, Sirius passes only half a degree south of the zenith; and, on this account, I have, for some time, looked upon that as the most proper place to make observations at, for this purpose.'

In 1761, the Royal Society sent Maskelyne to St Helena to observe a transit of Venus that would shed light on the scale of the solar system, in addition to determining the distance to the sun. He set sail on *Prince Henry*. During the voyage, he experimented with the determination of longitude by observation of the Moon's position using lunar tables produced by the German astronomer Tobias Mayer. Two years later, Maskelyne introduced this method into navigation by publishing *The British Mariners' Guide*. An English translation of Mayer's tables, with directions for their use, this cemented Maskelyne's future reputation. In 1765, Maskelyne became Astronomer Royal and published the first volume of the *Nautical Almanac,* continuing supervision of its production until his death.

Maskelyne arrived at St Helena in good time to find a suitable site for making observations. Unfortunately, the day of the transit of Venus was cloudy, and he was unable to complete the necessary measurements. He spent several months trying to make computations of Sirius, but concluded that his instruments were faulty; however, he compared the force of gravity at the island with that of Greenwich and used observations of the moon to gauge the size of the Earth.

The *Nautical Almanac* represents Nevil Maskelyne's enduring contribution to navigation. Personifying the lunar distance method of determining longitude, a legacy for St Helena was his calculation of the precise longitude of the island that hitherto had been unknown.

Outer Space and its manifestations in the stars and planets is an ancient fascination for natural philosophers, while the application of their study provided the means of making more accurate maps and navigating the vastness of oceans. In 1777, a brief visit was made to St Helena by a true pioneer in the scientific interest of the oceans, now vigorously pursued and commonly known as oceanography.

James Rennell was a British cartographer appointed at the age of twenty-one as surveyor-general of the EIC's dominions in Bengal. Responsible for preparing the first-ever survey of Bengal and the publication of the *Bengal Atlas,* he became known as the Father of Indian Geography. In 1777, Major Rennell returned to Britain with his family, taking passage from Calcutta on *Ashburnham*. During the long voyage around the Cape of Good Hope, he mapped and subsequently published a seminal work on what today is known as the Agulhas Current, and it is recognised as one of the first contributions to the science of oceanography. When *Ashburnham* arrived at St Helena, Mrs Rennell was so near her confinement that it was decided to remain on the island where their daughter Jane was born.

Captivated by the Atlantic currents that the homeward-bound vessels were compelled to cross, Rennell expanded his interests to ocean circulation generally. He helped survey portions of the deep ocean, writing papers on the Gulf Stream and North Atlantic Drift. His most important work, *Currents of the Atlantic Ocean,* was not significantly overtaken until 1936. His explanation of the northerly current found off the west-facing coast of the Bay of Biscay is called Rennell's Current. At Britain's prestigious National Oceanography Centre in Southampton – home base for today's world-leading Royal Research Ships – a lecture theatre bears his name. In recognition of his status, Major Rennell is buried next to David Livingstone at Westminster Abbey.

In the early 1820s, after Napoleon's death and burial on the island, the governor had a problem occupying the troops who were bored in their uneventful duty of guarding the tomb of the former emperor against attempts at bodysnatching by Republican loyalists. To this end, in 1823, he initiated a military institution for the education and advancement of the regiment's officers, which led to the building of an observatory on the heights of Ladder Hill.

Manuel Johnson was commissioned as a lieutenant with the EIC and assigned to an artillery unit stationed on St Helena. He developed an interest in astronomy that was encouraged by the governor. Johnson was given supervision of the observatory's construction and was subsequently made its superintendent. In 1835, as a result of observations made on St Helena, he published *A Catalogue of 606 Principal Fixed Stars in the Southern Hemisphere,* for which he won the Gold Medal of the Royal Astronomical Society.

When the island was transferred to the Crown in 1834, the commissioners recommended that the observatory should be abandoned despite the earlier important work by Johnson. This short-sightedness was remarked upon later by another eminent astronomer. In 1877, Professor David Gill and his wife were sent by the Royal Astronomical Society on an expedition to Ascension Island, necessitating a visit first to St Helena. Of the former observatory, Mrs Gill records: 'Fallen from its high estate, it is now the artillery mess-room, and in the recesses formed for the shutters of the openings through which Johnson's transit used to peep, they stow wineglasses and decanters, and under the dome they play billiards! ... I do not grudge the hospitable St Helena Mess their mess-room, but I do regret that so fine a site for an observatory is vacant.'

However, the Gills found the governor to be so kind, charming and persuasive that they were sorely tempted to make St Helena their observation station for the transit of Mars, instead of Ascension. Mrs Gill was sad when *Edinburgh Castle* was sighted, and she and her husband had to depart: 'St. Helena, now melting away in the distance, must be "The island of the Blessed" so fondly believed in and so earnestly sought for by the ancient mariners.'

In the latter stages of the epic five-year voyage of exploration and discovery by HMS *Beagle,* after leaving the Indian Ocean island of Mauritius and with a stopover at the Cape of Good Hope, in July 1836, the expedition stopped at St Helena for several days. It made an immediate impression on Charles Darwin:

This island, the forbidding aspect of which has been so often described, rises abruptly like a huge black castle from the ocean. Near the town, as if to complete nature's defence, small forts and guns fill every gap in the rugged rocks. The town runs up a flat and narrow valley; the houses look respectable and are interspersed with a very few green trees.

The lodgings Darwin took were close to Napoleon's tomb, a central situation convenient for explorations in all directions: 'During the four days I stayed here I wandered over the island from morning to night, and examined its geological history.' His observations enabled him to compare the characteristics of the landscape with his homeland. St Helena has been referred to as the lost county of England:

> Near the coast the rough lava is quite bare: in the central and higher parts, feldspathic rocks by their decomposition have produced a clayey soil, which, where not covered by vegetation, is stained in broad bands of many bright colours. At this season, the land moistened by constant showers, produces a singularly bright green pasture, which lower and lower down, gradually fades away and at last disappears. In latitude sixteen degrees, and at the trifling elevation of fifteen hundred feet, it is surprising to behold a vegetation possessing a character decidedly British.

Charles Darwin noted that the hills supported plantations of Scots firs; slopes covered with yellow-blooming gorse thickets; the banks of streams adorned with weeping willows, and hedges of blackberry producing copious soft fruit. He points out that the overwhelming majority of plant types on the island had been imported principally from England: 'Many of these English plants appear to flourish better than in their native country; some also from the opposite quarter of Australia succeed remarkably well. The many imported species must have destroyed some of the native kinds; and it is only on the highest and steepest ridges that the indigenous Flora is now predominant.'

The elevated plains of Longwood and Deadwood revealed a curious history of changes: 'Both plains, it is said, in former times were covered with wood, and were therefore called the Great Wood. So late as the year 1716 there were many trees, but in 1724 the old trees had mostly fallen; and as goats and hogs had been suffered to range about, all the young trees had been killed.' The plains eventually became covered with a fine sward, offering some 2,000 acres, then regarded as the best pasture on St Helena.

Of the built environment, Darwin adds: 'The English, or rather Welsh character of the scenery, is kept up by the numerous cottages and small white houses; some buried at the bottom of the deepest valleys, and others mounted on the crests of the lofty hills.'

The birds and insects were found to be as expected:

> I believe all the birds have been introduced within late years. Partridges and pheasants are tolerably abundant: the island is much too English not to be subject to strict game-laws. I was told of a more unjust sacrifice to such ordinances than I ever heard of even in England. The poor people formerly used to burn a plant, which grows on the coast-rocks, and export the soda from its ashes; but a peremptory order came out prohibiting this practice, and giving as a reason that the partridges would have nowhere to build!

The complicated geological disturbances revealed scenes of high interest for Darwin: 'According to my views, St Helena has existed as an island from a very remote epoch; some obscure proofs, however, of the elevation of the land are still extant. I believe that the central and highest peaks form parts of the rim of a great crater, the southern half of which has been entirely removed by the waves of the sea: there is, moreover, an external wall of black basaltic rocks, like the coast-mountains of Mauritius, which are older than the central volcanic streams.'

An observation by Charles Darwin concerning his time on St Helena has a particular modern resonance for the island today:

> The only inconvenience I suffered during my walks was from the impetuous winds. One day I noticed a curious circumstance; standing on the edge of a plain, terminated by a great cliff of about a thousand feet in depth, I saw at a distance of a few yards right to windward, some tern, struggling against a very strong breeze, whilst, where I stood, the air was quite calm. Approaching close to the brink, where the current seemed to be deflected upwards from the face of the cliff, I stretched out my arm, and immediately felt the full force of the wind: an invisible barrier, two yards in width, separated perfectly calm air from a strong blast.

Darwin was much taken with the island: 'I so much enjoyed my rambles among the rocks and mountains of St Helena, that I felt almost sorry on the morning of the fourteenth to descend to the town. Before noon I was on board, and the *Beagle* made sail [for Ascension].'

One hundred and fifty years after Charles Darwin completed his epic voyage, a research ship owned and operated by the UK's Natural Environment Research Council, and named the Royal Research Ship (RRS) *Charles Darwin,* carried out another global circumnavigation that lasted three and a half years. The then state-of-the-art oceanographic vessel supported some two dozen scientific teams charged with addressing some of the fundamental problems of modern oceanography and marine biology, studying topics as diverse as the causes of El Nino, deep sea currents in the Indian Ocean and the speed with which the Indian subcontinent moves towards Asia.

In recognition of the contribution major historic scientific figures have made to the understanding of many sciences, to inspire latter-day proponents and help impress on the public the endeavours all such commitments still require, modern research ships are often given names of figures such as Charles Darwin. An earlier vessel that RRS *Charles Darwin* was built to replace was RRS *Shackleton.*

In the latter half of the 1950s, this redoubtable little ship helped serve the logistical needs of British scientific bases in the Antarctic. At the close of the workable season in the southern continent, and on passage back to the UK, while at Montevideo in Uruguay, *Shackleton* was co-opted by the Colonial Office for an unusual assignment. It was one that found her destined for St Helena, via her even more isolated island neighbour to the south, Tristan da Cunha.

To this remote island, a British freighter had transported a complete sewerage system for installation at the only small settlement, Edinburgh. The ship had lain for many days, unable to discharge due to adverse sea conditions. When the charter period expired, the ship made for Montevideo and offloaded the cargo. *Shackleton* was given the task of fulfilling the delivery. An uneventful easterly passage of 1,000 miles ended with a successful transfer of the plant materials ashore.

Tristan da Cunha and St Helena had long-established links, and *Shackleton* was requested to convey a dozen Tristan inhabitants to St Helena – described as mostly young, very shy and timorous – to visit their relatives. It was to be an unlooked-for and serendipitous event that brought yet another ocean-wandering little ship to the environs of St Helena.

In 1836, the influential Prussian geographer, naturalist and explorer Alexander von Humbolt initiated an international survey of terrestrial magnetism. He asked the Royal Society if Britain would set up magnetic stations in its colonies.

St Helena was chosen as approximate to the point of least intensity of magnetic force on the globe. Lt John Henry Lefroy RA was appointed, with three additional staff, to set up a 'Mag. & Met.' – Magnetical and Meteorological – Observatory. They were sent on the Antarctic survey ships HMSs *Erebus* and *Terror,* under Captain Sir James Clark Ross RN who was also taking magnetic readings.

Captain Ross was an Englishman who, by this time, was considered the most experienced polar officer in the world. In 1831, he had successfully located the north magnetic pole. He sailed south for Antarctica in the autumn of 1839, in command of *Erebus* and *Terror.* The aim was to find the south magnetic pole. This was to be part of Britain's contribution to an international year of cooperation, where European nations would set up magnetic observatories around the world, coordinating readings on fixed dates and comparing results.

On St Helena, Lefroy chose Longwood, the place of former incarceration of Napoleon Bonaparte, stating that 'the soil around is deep, producing no sensible effect on the magnet'. The importance of the work at Longwood is exemplified by one five-year experiment in which 'the hourly declinometer readings measuring magnetic variation were *inter alia,* compared with records made by navigators at St Helena since 1610, a comparison made possible because its anchorage was so small that the data would refer to exactly the same place. This revealed that lines of terrestrial magnetism had undergone a 'wholly unsuspected' 30-degree change over a period of 236 years.'

This was claimed to be 'one of the most important theoretical conclusions made from the Colonial observations' and which 'must find a place in any physical theory to explain the phenomenon of the earth's magnetism'. Despite pleas for the observatory to be retained, it was closed on the ten-year deadline.

Proponents of other scientific disciplines have continued to visit St Helena; one of the most recent being Steve Owens. Invited in 2012 by the island's Tourism Association to assess the darkness of St Helena's night skies, in his capacity with the International Dark Sky Association the data he collected indicated that the island qualified for the highest rating – 'Gold Tier' status, and explained: 'Under such dark skies the Milky Way can be seen stretching from horizon to horizon in an arc overhead and the heavens are studded with thousands of stars and many nebulae, including the dramatic Magellanic clouds not visible from far northern latitudes. Indeed its location at sixteen degrees south of the equator means that virtually every constellation is on display at some time throughout the year.'

Once the preserve of professional scientists, it is hoped now that the growing trend in dark sky tourism will encourage an additional eclectic mix of visitors to journey to St Helena.

CHAPTER 11

A Force for Freedom

Slavery in the British Empire was abolished from 1834, but it remained in America. Slave ships continued to operate between West Africa and the Americas, often passing close to St Helena. In 1840, the British government based a naval station on the island to suppress this trade. The specially formed West African Squadron supported the newly established Vice Admiralty Court on St Helena for the trial of captured ships. In the following decade, many such vessels were brought to the island, to be sold and broken up.

The erstwhile slaves were fed, clothed and retained at the Liberated African Depot at Rupert's Valley. Returned to health, they voyaged to the British West Indies for employment. In this period, 10,000 liberated Africans were sent mainly to these islands. During initial recovery and before reshipment, those able to work were engaged on public works. Others remained on St Helena as servants or in private service.

An observer who boarded a captured slaver off the island notes: 'The vessel, scarcely one-hundred tons berthen at most, contains perhaps little short of a thousand souls, which have been closely packed, for many weeks together, in the hottest and most polluted of atmospheres.' The first bishop to ever visit St Helena – the bishop of Cape Town, Robert Gray – visited the depot after it had accepted a new influx of casualties: 'There were not less than six-hundred poor souls in it ... of these more than three hundred were in hospital; some affected with dreadful opthalmia; others with severe rheumatism, others with dysentery, the number of deaths in the week being twenty-one.'

The depot and ships of the cruising naval squadron brought prosperity to St Helena that was timely in reducing the distress resulting from the island's transfer to the Crown in 1834. One of the first engagements of the squadron was made by HMS *Water Witch,* which seized a slaver off the Angolan coast. *Water Witch*'s second officer James Wilcox took command of the captured ship for the thirteen-day passage to St Helena.

Water Witch was custom built in 1832 as a 30-m racing yacht. Acquired two years later by the Navy, she patrolled south of the equator in the anti-slaving campaign. Prolific in capturing and sending to St Helena forty-two slave ships and freeing over 3,000 Africans during her lengthy commission, she has been attributed as singlehandedly capturing more vessels than the whole of the United States Africa Squadron put together. No other British vessel came close to her achievements.

At the peak of her success, *Water Witch* was commanded by Lt Henry James Masson. He adopted an aggressive approach towards slavers. Recruiting a crew of up to seventy, they came from Britain, America, Germany, Africa, the East Indies and St Helena. The Africans were recruited for their natural immunity to malaria that was beneficial for landing excursions.

Liberated Africans remained on St Helena, and they had a great affinity with the ship that had freed them. However, they generally stayed at the bottom of the social strata as uneducated labourers and paupers, often dying in obscurity.

There were also physical and economic legacies from abolition. The breaking up of slave ships brought in wood, iron, building materials and firewood. The naval crews were extremely profitable to the island. They were not allowed to land on the African coast, making St Helena an exclusive retail haven. Jamestown was notorious for 'fleecing' passing visitors, a quality that sustained the economy for many years.

An unforeseen consequence, disastrous for St Helena, resulted from these humanitarian efforts of liberating slaves by the island that, historically, had employed a 'benign' form of slavery. In 1840, a slave ship from Brazil was deconstructed and her timbers deposited in Jamestown. Unbeknownst, it was infested with termites. Initially, they stealthily destroyed books, clothes and furniture before focusing on the wooden structures of buildings. Eventually, Jamestown was destroyed and cost £60,000 to rebuild. The insects continued their slow spread, inflicting wider damage to buildings and trees across the island.

The West African Squadron left St Helena in 1864, although the establishment at Rupert's Valley remained open for another ten years. Today, a tall marble monument to sailors who served on *Water Witch* stands in the secluded and quiet park of Castle Gardens in Jamestown.

CHAPTER 12

Harpoons at a Venture

For two centuries, whaling was one of St Helena's main sources of income but, like the flax industry, the whale fishery had a fitful start before dominating the island economy until it died amid forlorn hopes of recovery. St Helena's role in the whaling industry has been described as 'more than an episode in the island's story: it also epitomizes the southern whale fishery's intricate international history.'

St Helena was involved in southern whaling from its outset in the 1780s, when English whalers were extending operations into the South Atlantic from their customary grounds around Greenland. The recent American War of Independence had robbed Britain of its main source of sperm whale oil, not from its own whalers, but from the Quaker whaling community of Nantucket Island, Massachusetts. These whalers had developed methods of processing catches aboard ship, allowing northern whalemen to exploit southern waters. To safeguard supplies, the British government offered whalemen financial aid to exploit the southern fishery.

The French Wars of Napoleon now added the hazards of conflict to those of whaling, but St Helena gained, as all the other ports in southern latitudes were closed against them, making Jamestown a welcome base for whalers seeking 'refreshment and health'. In 1859, an American whaleman later recorded: 'Jamestown is a sailor's paradise: there is neither lack of women nor wine.'

To exploit the gift of St Helena's war-induced strategic position, its governor, Robert Brooke, proposed: 'a depot on the island, where the ships employed in the fishery should bring their cargoes, and unload them there, which would relieve them from the necessity of returning so frequently to Europe. The cargoes thus deposited [would] be carried home in the ships employed to bring out the annual supplies.'

Funding of such a project would only be forthcoming if local investment was made. The governor sent his plan to reputable merchants in Jamestown. It was rejected due to the cost of constructing the necessary buildings.

In 1805, an observer on St Helena recorded:

Whales are seen playing about the island in such numbers that it is supposed the Southern whale fishery might be carried on here with great advantage as it certainly might with safety and without difficulty, in seas which are never obstructed with ice nor ruffled with hurricanes. This circumstance may, in future, constitute a source of wealth and trade to the island itself.

Neither Jamestown traders nor London capitalists were tempted to invest but, as events transpired, the strict shipping conditions in place during Napoleon's six-year incarceration on St Helena may have hamstrung any island-based whaling enterprise. The inertia of local merchants had the effect of denying the island's storage facilities, creating a constant shortage in its own stocks of whale oil. Whalers' casual sales were so unreliable that supplies were ordered from the EIC's agent at the Cape. The situation has been described as 'sending coals to Newcastle'. Yet, demand rose considerably after Napoleon's death in 1821.

The contribution shipping was making to St Helena's prosperity was burgeoning. Peace in Europe, the opening of trade with China and Jamestown's status as a 'Free Port' from 1826 greatly increased the number of vessels using the island. Whalemen were liberal with their spending, especially when homeward bound. English whalers had left Pacific waters to the Americans, preferring the Indian Ocean. In 1829, twenty English and two American whalers visited St Helena.

Dramatic changes in the southern whale fishery were about to hit the island. By 1855, the vast majority of visiting whalers were from America. In context, Jamestown dealt with over a thousand other ships that year. The apparent reversal of whaling fortunes was largely due to Britain switching from whale oil to coal gas and paraffin, while America's pioneering rural society still provided an expanding market for whale products.

Economically, American whalers brought threefold benefit: for bringing stores; for trans-shipping whale products and for their free-spending crews. Records in a *St Helena Almanac* show that, in 1856, whalers brought a quarter of island imports and took almost all its exports. St Helena was commonly used by whalers as a post office and was thus a wished-for port. Letters left for crew were collected and others delivered for island residents serving on ships in the Indian Ocean. Yankee whalers soon had additional causes to appreciate St Helena, as a haven during the American Civil War, from the Confederate raider *Alabama*.

A classic study of St Helena by J. Melliss gives an island view of the industry:

At least 60 or 70 [American whalers] call at the island every year, rendezvous for refitting, re-provisioning, and trans-shipping their oil to those vessels which may be homeward bound, about the month of October ... The local whaling grounds extend from 30 to 180 miles off the Island, but the vessels are constantly seen cruising, close to the land from April to July, and whales have even been taken within a few miles of the roadstead. Beyond the circulation of money which these vessels occasion, the St Helenians derive no profit whatever from the source of wealth, which lies at their very doors. One or more whaling ships have been fitted out from the Island, but the spirit of enterprise succumbed to the misfortunes which befell such attempt.

In 1875, the barque *Elizabeth* had been fitted out as a whale ship by St Helena's leading merchants, Solomon, Moss, Gideon & Company. Manned by islanders, some of whom had crewed the American whalers, the venture lasted two seasons. This well-meaning enterprise was begun at a bad time, as the South Atlantic whale fishery was then in advanced decline. Eventually, the wider whaling fleet's decline led to its withdrawal in 1896: a serious blow as it had given employment to a significant number of islanders and raised large sums from the sale of local produce.

It was the scarcity of right whales that convinced one visitor that St Helena's role as a 'great centre of the whaling was doomed'. Meanwhile, the occasional whaler kept islanders' hopes alive that the Americans would return. It is believed that the last St Helenian whaleman to be paid off at Jamestown was Mr Harris, in 1908.

In 1911, seven whalers shipped some 4,600 barrels of oil, together with bone, to America. In the following year, nine whalers called in for coal bunkers. An American whaler visited in 1916; Norwegian whalers did likewise in 1924 and 1925. Whales made their final contribution to the St Helena economy in 1960 when a massive Norwegian factory ship left Jamestown for a last hunt in Antarctica.

Whaling has left St Helena with positive legacies. Relics of the old whaling days would have been brought back to the island. The breaking up or rebuilding of condemned whalers was a major money-spinner. The dolphin fishery used tackle and terminology from whaling, and whaling songs continued in popularity as an enduring echo to such a significant part of St Helena's heritage.

CHAPTER 13

Merchantable Quality

Saul Solomon and Richard Prince have respectively been referred to as St Helena's 'Merchant King' and 'Merchant Prince'. Add Samuel Hopewell to these names, and St Helena is able to boast a trio of historic merchant supremos who have left their legacy on the island to this day.

Long before Napoleon arrived for incarceration, Solomon had founded a business that was to wield great and lasting influence. Born in 1776 in the south of England, he was twenty and making a passage to India when he became ill and was landed at St Helena. He stayed.

After several years of military service on the island, he opened a general store and boarding house, the success of which marked the start of his rise in 'trade'. A decade later, he went into partnership with an established wealthy merchant. Much of his success is owed to Napoleon's exile. This gave rise to a doubling of the population and consequent creation of wealth and opportunities, which Solomon could exploit. This spanned both luxury trades and commercial markets.

Eventually, his premises became venues for the societies of both the governor and the former emperor. These became centres that were evidently rife with gossip and intrigue, earning the proprietor a reputation of less-than complete loyalty to the government, and he was an assumed admirer of Napoleon. This did not, however, prevent him 'overcharging' Napoleon who had grumbled at the 12s price per pound for macaroni. Likewise, in general, he was keen on driving a bargain on receipt of merchandise deliveries.

Solomon was one of the first to register as a shipping agent, which he did in 1832, becoming consular agent for France the following year. In years ahead, consular status was secured for many countries. At one period, agents in Jamestown represented at least fourteen governments. During the four-decade period when St Helena became pivotal for the South Atlantic whaling industry, with huge numbers of ships calling each year, consuls from America and Norway were residents on the island. America's consuls played a vital role in the industry, but they brought other benefits. St Helena's trade with America by the 1870s was third in importance after Britain and South Africa and owed much to the enterprise of the consuls. One example found the import from a company in New Orleans of exceptionally fine American red cypress wood as a timber best suited to resist the ravages of termites.

Consuls also encouraged whalers to import goods at rates that were evidently beneficial to the island community, as observed: oil, timber, oilcake for cattle, oats and such like could be purchased cheap in America and imported by schooner at reasonable freight charges. Other contacts led, for example, to a two-month expedition from Cleveland Museum on the *Blossom* and, in 1928, the first ever visit of an American luxury liner. During the 1930s, several visits a year were made by American–South African liners at St Helena.

On the transfer of St Helena from the EIC to the Crown, the Solomon empire continued to flourish. Old company landed families sold out at great loss, enabling merchants like Solomon to profit and prosper. During the founder's lifetime, despite the social disadvantages of being 'in trade', Solomon & Company became stalwarts of the Establishment, and the Church.

Saul Solomon died in England in 1852, but his wish to be buried on St Helena was honoured through the enterprise and nerve of his daughter. Embarking on the ship *Camperdown*, unbeknownst to all onboard, she had brought her father's corpse. The ensuing journey was of great stress, for fear that if the fact became known by the crew, her father would be summarily despatched overboard.

Solomon's remains were interred in Jamestown's lower burial ground. The *St Helena Herald* records: 'The concourse of people attending the funeral was very large and many seemed deeply affected ... while the poor appeared most deeply to lament the loss of one whose kindness to them was almost proverbial, there were mourners there of every rank and society.' Solomon & Company were later to proclaim its historic pre-eminence of the consular role at Jamestown by calling its hotel – still extant today – 'The Consulate'.

The Solomon dynasty at St Helena ended in 1974 when their businesses were 'nationalised' by the St Helena government.

*

In 1813, Richard Prince, who was a merchant from the Cape, journeyed from Cape Town to St Helena on *Mornington* in order to enforce payment of debts overdue to his London firm from Saul Solomon. He also stayed, setting up a rival concern that went on to trade for some ninety years. To help with the business, he enlisted the services of his four brothers.

Prince quickly appreciated the island's commercial potential as the East Indiamen's sole port of call on homeward passage. In business, he was to follow Solomon's tried and tested example. He was not to enjoy the fruits of his success for long, dying in 1838 and passing the firm to his nephew, Samuel Hopewell. He had first come to St Helena as a teenager to work for his uncle. Hopewell's character has been described as epitomising the honest, thrusting Victorian businessman who astutely kept a finger on the pulse of the commercial world by judicious visits to London. He eventually retired and returned to England, handing the family business to his son Richard Prince Hopewell.

In the 1860s, the sharp decline in shipping as steamers, the Overland Route to India, and the Suez Canal, made St Helena progressively more remote from the world's shipping lanes. The local economy slumped severely, and competition between Jamestown tradesmen grew fierce. Solomons moved to monopolise trade in the port and was to outlast the business initiated originally by the 'Merchant Prince'.

CHAPTER 14

Coals to St Helena

In the heyday of sail, numbers of ships calling at St Helena routinely exceeded 1,000 annually. The island was cherished as a mid-ocean depot by homeward-bound East Indiamen and as the general hub of South Atlantic sailing routes. However, when sail gave way to steam, the routes of which were governed neither by wind nor by current but generally the shortest distance between ports of call, the notion that St Helena would automatically become a major coaling station was misplaced. Jamestown did fulfil a bunkering role for warships, merchantmen and liners, but in a relatively minor capacity, as steamers rarely had reason to make the island a destination.

Cited as a possible contributing factor in the critical early days of steam were the notorious charges of the Jamestown tradesmen that discouraged not only many sailing ships but even the steamers of Union-Castle Line. They held a mail contract with St Helena, but still preferred to coal at Madeira or the Cape Verde Islands. It has been conjectured that the main agent on St Helena, Solomon & Company, may have imported coal for household use and to have held speculative stocks for steamers. Later, the Admiralty delivered stocks to meet naval needs.

The P&O paddle steamer *Pekin* is recorded as an early steamer to visit St Helena, arriving unexpectedly in December 1846, but no coaling was recorded. In 1849, HMSS *Geyser* brought the Anglican Bishop Gray from Cape Town. Three years later, regular steam communication began with the General Screw Steam Shipping Company. Also in 1852, the island was graced by none other than the SS *Great Britain*, in desperate need of 500 tons of coal. Steaming against wind and current, she had run short of fuel 700 miles from the Cape of Good Hope while on passage to Australia and had to sail some 1,100 miles to St Helena for supplies.

A passenger, Edward Towle, describes the outcome: 'As there is very little coal we are obliged to use wood.' One hundred tons was procured from shore at £5.17.0 per ton; several hundred tons of wood at about £3 per ton, and one hundred tons from HMS *Penelope*. Three months later, USS *Mississippi*, carrying Commodore Perry to Japan on a trade mission, took on coal 'as a measure rather of prudence than necessity'.

Since 1840, the Royal Navy's anti-slavery patrol had increasingly used Ascension and St Helena, where a Vice Admiralty Court had been established. By 1854, the thirteen vessels of the West African Squadron included at least seven steamers. Although their needs were largely met elsewhere, nevertheless, the earlier plight of the SS *Great Britain* and other steam-assisted sailing ships encouraged those on St Helena who thought it worthwhile investing in coal, despite steamers' poor performance, mechanical unreliability and cargo space given over to carrying bunkers. Jamestown had advantages over its rivals. The Cape Verde Islands were Portuguese and Ascension, at its exposed anchorage, suffered from rollers – waves that are un-noticeable at sea but that can generate major breakers when reaching shallow water. James Bay offered effective shelter.

On the Jamestown Wharf, hard beneath the cliffs that overlook the landing steps, a coal yard was eventually established. As there was no quayside, everything had to be brought ashore by lighters, making operations doubly hazardous. Remnants of iron rings set into the cliff, for pulling up coal bags, still exist. Records of 1854 show that some 550 tons of coal were imported from Britain.

The Union Steamship Company's monthly Cape mail run was inaugurated by the Royal Mail Steamer *Dane,* with a daily coal consumption of 7 tons, calling at St Helena on the homeward voyage in October 1857.

The governor's annual reports to the colonial office reveal the changing fortunes of St Helena's coaling station:

1873: 'The situation of St Helena in mid-ocean (sighted by all ships from India, and a very large number from Australia) renders it a most important position for Imperial purposes as a coaling station and depot for vessels of war, and it would be highly desirable that it should not be allowed to fall into insignificance, more particularly in the event of hostilities the sinking of one ship in the Suez Canal (either by accident or design) might effectually close that passage. Two or three steamers stationed here would intercept the whole of the returning trade from the East.'

1914: April: 'German South Atlantic Squadron re-coaled at Jamestown ... Only one shipment of coal was imported by the local contractor, owing to the arrival of Admiralty colliers during the last four months of the year. Five whalers put in for bunker fuel.'

The German South Atlantic Squadron was destroyed in December 1914 at the Battle of the Falklands.

1924: 'Two Admiralty colliers paid 1/- per ton import duty. A large consignment of anthracite coal was imported for use in two of the flax mills.'

1966–68: 'Coal not listed among imports.'

Above: RMS *St Helena* at Portland, England, preparing for Voyage 60 (south).

Left: Puppies bound for the South Atlantic view loading in the 'tween deck.

Loading general stores.

A bracing game on deck while crossing the Bay of Biscay.

Ongoing maintenance at sea; greasing the crane wires.

Right: Letting go the port anchor during berthing manoeuvres at Santa Cruz, Tenerife.

Below: The forward mooring party secure the ship alongside at Santa Cruz.

Left: Travelling with the ship, the German film company Little Sparrow capture a heavy lift bound for St Helena.

Below: Taking on board bunker fuel from a barge at Santa Cruz.

Above left: Touching up the hull paintwork while alongside.

Above right: Vital unseen work takes place underwater at the stern of the ship.

Right: The shore-leave board keeps shore-goers officially informed.

The onboard 'Castle Curry Cup' cricket match attracts participants of all ages.

The chief officer regularly inspects the cargo spaces and tightens up lashings slackened by movement of the ship.

At the Equator, the time-honoured 'Crossing the Line' ceremony is conducted with gusto.

Traditional position fixing by celestial navigation, using a sextant and nautical tables.

Left: A balmy night feast on the after deck.

Below: Bringing the ship to anchor at Ascension Island.

Above: Discharging containers onto powered barges, off Georgetown, Ascension.

Right: At Ascension, the puppy heads for home to the island's dentist.

Left: Passengers visit Comfortless Cove, a site where fever-ridden sailors were quarantined in the mid-nineteenth century.

Below: The transfer launch from the island is kept busy during the one-day call at Ascension.

Off-duty staff from the engineering department savour the coastal passage of Ascension...

...and passengers marvel at Boatswain Bird Island.

A much-anticipated occasion: St Helena is sighted.

The chief officer takes a check bearing on the approach to James Bay, St Helena.

Right: RMS *St Helena* once again at anchor, off Jamestown, St Helena.

Below: Discharging proceeds apace.

All cargo is taken ashore from barges at the Wharf.

St Helenians take up their periodic roles as cargo stevedores aboard *St Helena*...

...transferred by launch.

Physically disadvantaged passengers avoid
the inclined accommodation ladder steps by
using the ship's 'air taxi'.

Above: A pause in cargo operations.

Left and overleaf (top): The Caterpillar bulldozer begins its final journey to St Helena ...

Below: The mobile shore crane carries out the final lift from the moored-off barge to shore.

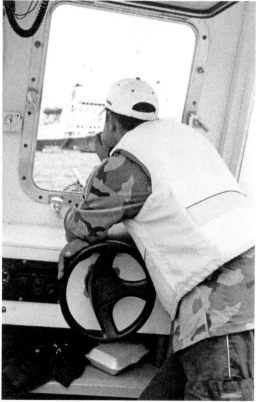

Above: Containers are unstuffed for customs clearance.

Left: The liberty launch keeps up a steady service between ship and shore.

St Helena departs on the shuttle service to Ascension and back.

The final destination of Voyage 60 (south): Cape Town, South Africa.

CHAPTER 15

Stamps of Approval

Although St Helena was frequently visited by ships of the EIC, prior to 1815, letters bore no external indication of their association with the island, as there was no post office at that time. Letters were either left under large stones or handed directly to the captains of ships. Later, it was arranged that they could be left at the government secretary's office to await the next ship.

The first Post Office on St Helena opened in 1815. Thereafter, all letters carried by mail packet had to have an official Post Office mark or stamp. The UK Post Office began issuing prepaid stamps in the UK in 1840, but it was not until 1856 that the first stamp of St Helena was issued, a sixpenny blue, portraying Queen Victoria.

St Helena regularly issues commemorative and omnibus stamps. All aspects of St Helena's long and diverse history are pictorially recalled in its stamps, not least its rich maritime heritage and associations.

CHAPTER 16

A Green and Pleasant Alcatraz

St Helena has a notable historical reputation as a prison, a place of insular yet open incarceration that has earned it the reputation of being 'humane'. Napoleon Bonaparte, after his defeat at the Battle of Waterloo, lived at Longwood for six years prior to his death.

After the Zulu war in South Africa, the Zulu Chief Dinizulu was banished to St Helena in 1889 following his conviction for high treason against the British Crown. Condemned to serve a ten-year sentence, he lived a comfortable existence on the island, learning to play the piano and organ, fathering seven children, converting to Christianity and being baptised and confirmed by the bishop.

During the South African Boer War, St Helena was used as a POW camp. Indeed, the island was the first place to receive Boer prisoners. However, the camp was quickly overwhelmed by numbers, and new camps were established in India, Bermuda and Ceylon.

More than 5,000 prisoners were held on St Helena, camped on 'Deadwood Plain' and 'Broad Bottom'. Over 500 were the first to be landed in April 1900 from SS *Milwaukee*. Further prisoners arrived onboard *Lake Erie, Bavarian* and *Mongolian*. More were to arrive in 1902 on *Orient* and *Britannia*.

Prior to the arrival of the prisoners, the governor of St Helena, R. A. Sterndale, published the proclamation: 'His Excellency expresses the hope that the population will treat the prisoners of war with that courtesy and consideration which should be extended to all men who have fought bravely for what they considered the cause of their country, and will help in repressing any unseemly demonstrations which individuals might exhibit.'

Expecting harshness, rudeness and ill feeling among the inhabitants, the prisoners discovered from the proclamation that they might anticipate courtesy and respect instead. These they were accorded from the crowds of islanders who had congregated to observe their transit to the camp prepared for them some miles distant over hilly terrain.

The Boer War has been described as a period of sustained and spontaneous creation of folk art, considered one of the most productive and creative times in the cultural history of the Afrikaner. St Helena's Boer prisoners made their own contribution. At the Deadwood Camp, craftsmen held a five-day exhibition of works, including model carts, carved boxes, pipes and walking sticks, all made using makeshift tools. Some of the folk art features in the Anglo-Boer War Museum in Bloemfontein, South Africa.

In May 1901, at Jamestown, two Boers swam to a Russian ship moored in the harbour, but they were not permitted to board and were later recaptured. In the same year, in South Africa, all ships arriving at St Helena from the Cape were under strict quarantine regulations. No passengers other than those destined for the island were allowed to disembark. No cargo was landed, and there was no parcel post, all of which contributed to a serious loss of trade.

When peace was proclaimed and repatriation approached, the governor was addressed by grateful prisoners: 'In the first place we want to express our heartfelt thanks for the kindness and consideration shown to the prisoners of war. The kindness shown to one and all by all the people of the island, with a few exceptions, is a fact that will be long remembered and cherished by them as a bright spark in the gloomy days of captivity at St Helena.'

Not all of the prisoners survived to return home. One hundred and sixty-seven former Boers are buried in a well-maintained hillside cemetery at Knollcombes. Ages range from sixteen to sixty-one. In 1913, the Union Government sent over two granite monuments, upon which all the names are inscribed.

CHAPTER 17

Royal Interest

It has been speculated that Prince Rupert of the Rhine (1619–82) was the first royal to visit St Helena, considered to have done so on a voyage home from India. No contemporary documents evidently exist, but no other explanation has been offered for the naming of Rupert's Bay, adjacent to Jamestown. Rupert is cited as being the most talented Royalist commander of the English Civil War. In later life, he held a series of British naval commands and, among other achievements, became the first governor of the Hudson's Bay Company.

In 1840, the Prince of Joinville arrived on the French frigate *La Belle Poule* to return the body of Napoleon to France, in what became known as the *Retour des cendres* – the return of the 'ashes'.

The island's first officially recorded royal visit was in 1860 by Queen Victoria's second son, Prince Alfred who, as a serving naval officer, arrived on the steam frigate HMS *Euryalus* while returning home from South Africa. As part of the formalities of this one-day visit, a deputation by the inhabitants addressed the prince, expressing their loyalty and enterprise:

> we regard ourselves as contributing to the strength of the British Empire by the advantages with which Nature has endowed our island. The trade wind blowing constantly over us, the depth of water and safe anchorage of our harbour, the numerous springs of purest water afforded by our mountain slopes, the fertility of our cultivated valleys, – all these have combined to obtain for our island the title of 'The Inn of the Ocean'.

Prince Alfred also presented new colours to HM's St Helena Regiment.

In 1880, the widow of Napoleon III, Empress Eugenie, arrived on her way from a visit to the grave of her son in South Africa. She was entertained by the governor, but no festivities marked her call, out of respect for her deep mourning. In the same year, Prince Henry of Prussia visited on a German frigate.

Queen Victoria's third son, Prince Arthur, the Duke of Connaught, visited in 1910 on HMS *Balmoral Castle*.

In 1925, The Prince of Wales, later to become Edward VIII, arrived at St Helena aboard HMS *Repulse.* In a speech on his arrival in Jamestown, as well as paying respects to

Napoleon's memory, he celebrated St Helena's loyalty to the empire and acknowledged the importance of the flax industry 'on which much of your material prosperity depends'.

The only reigning monarch to visit St Helena was George VI. This was in 1947 when the king, accompanied by Queen Elizabeth, Princess Elizabeth and Princess Margaret, was travelling on HMS *Vanguard* during the Royal Tour of South Africa. Having looked around a dilapidated Longwood House, almost destroyed by termites, the king signed the visitors' book and expressed his concern at the building's perilous state and his hope that the French government would do what was necessary to restore the historic former residence of Napoleon.

A narrative compiled from the official diary of the voyage around the world of the newly commissioned Royal Yacht *Britannia* in 1956/57, from which HRH the Duke of Edinburgh visited St Helena, subsequent to a visit to Tristan da Cunha, records aspects of the occasion:

ST. HELENA: Tuesday 22 January
When we anchored at 9.30am however, the sea was almost flat but there was still enough swell at the landing pier to make it hazardous for motorboats to go alongside. We therefore transferred to the island boats which went into the stone steps stern-first and, with the aid of hanging ropes, we jumped ashore as the opportunity came.

Going up the mountain on the way inland to look at the remainder of the island, many of us stopped to look giddily down the Jacob's Ladder, an almost vertical stone stairway down the side of the valley. Others, more energetic, climbed its 699 steps and having reached the top had the fun of seeing the island boys, in exchange for shillings, slide down the four hundred feet drop sitting on the handrails.

His Royal Highness gave a dinner party on board in the evening and, when the guests had all embarked into shore boats, we sailed at 11pm.

While on the island, Prince Philip opened the new playground in Lower Market Street. Today the facility is known as the Duke of Edinburgh Playground.

HRH Prince Andrew visited St Helena on HMS *Herald* in 1984, as a member of the armed forces, in recognition of the island's 150th anniversary as a Crown colony. A song of welcome was composed, and there were many celebrations of marching and singing. A dance was held at the Paramount Cinema and a performance of 'Fibre', a musical produced by the children from the island's schools. St Helena's new senior school is named after Prince Andrew, in honour of the visit.

Prince Andrew is also Patron of the Saint Helena National Trust, the aims of which are to preserve the island's environmental and cultural heritage. Key examples are the Millennium Forest, a 250-hectare area of replanting to restore part of what was the Great Wood, the conservation of the St Helena plover, the island's national bird known locally as the wirebird and the restoration of High Knoll Fort near Jamestown.

HRH the Princess Royal visited the island in 2002 to celebrate 'Q5' – the quincentenary of St Helena. Travelling on RMS *St Helena*, Princess Anne came ashore by the island launch *Gannet 2*. Among official duties was the presentation of twenty-two Queen's Golden Jubilee Medals to members of the St Helena Emergency Services.

CHAPTER 18

The Victorian Internet
Comes Calling

Advances in technology and the introduction of innovation are spurred for many reasons, not least war.

At the time of the Anglo-Zulu War of 1879, it took nearly three weeks for a message to travel from Southern Africa via steamer to the Cape Verde Islands and, on by telegraph, to London. As this remained the case at the outbreak of the Second Boer War in 1899, a faster and more direct route was urgently needed.

The Eastern Telegraph Company contracted the Telegraph Construction and Maintenance Company to manufacture and lay the necessary cables that were to link Cape Town – St Helena – Ascension and St Vincent in the Cape Verde Islands. Messages could then be routed over pre-existing cables to Britain. The Maintenance Company steamship *John Pender* carried out sounding surveys at St Helena, preparatory to the cable being laid.

The cable ship CS *Anglia* laid the first stage from Cape Town to St Helena, a length of over 2,000 nautical miles. While this ship returned to Britain for more cable, CS *Seine* laid the onward section to Ascension. *Anglia* laid the section from Ascension to St Vincent. The whole task was completed in February 1900, only four months after the start of the war.

In advance of the completion of the cable, a United States government publication stated: 'The connection by cable with the "mother country" will be the greatest boon ever conferred upon St Helena, for the reason that hundreds of merchant sailing ships from the East, which under existing arrangements go out of their way to call at the Brazils, Cape Verde and the West Indies for orders, will avail themselves of this station.'

To the inhabitants of St Helena, the coming of the cable has been likened to a Victorian internet. Its virtues were publicised by the Eastern Telegraph Company: 'The Cable connecting this Colony with Cape Town has been successfully laid and the Public are hereby Notified – that messages can now be transmitted from this Colony to Great Britain, Europe, America, Africa, etc., via Cape Town. The charge per word from St Helena is laid down in the Tariff which can be seen at the Post Office, or at the Transmitting Station, Rupert's Valley.'

*

It was a direct military threat from seaward that inspired the first visual telegraph system in the southern hemisphere – on St Helena. In 1803, war was resumed with France. As an isolated and strategic outpost, St Helena was vulnerable to surprise attack. Fundamental to its defence was rapid and appropriate deployment of the island's small garrison of troops. Early warning of ships approaching from seaward was vital to the command based in Jamestown. St Helena's rugged terrain was a challenge to runners dispatched across the island. Such delays could be catastrophic.

The island's new governor, Colonel Robert Patton, devised a simple, effective and cheap system of communication, of which he was able to report:

> [it is] composed of a frame of wood and balls, because our stations are generally upon heights having the sky behind which renders such objects distinctly visible ... With only four balls, one hundred different signals can be distinctly made, in the numerary manner, in that the system is a species of communication in cipher ... In darkness, the day signals were represented by a system of lanterns. The stations were manned around the clock.

The efficacy of the system impressed contemporaries: 'An enemy could not easily land here by surprise, for there are signals so placed all over the island, as to give instant notice of the approach of vessels to any part of the coast.' The establishment of such telegraph systems, and the incalculable advantages and security attached to them, enabled later evaluation: 'In the tactics of worldwide marine warfare culminating in the Battle of Trafalgar, St Helena had played its role – another story waiting to be told – in which the quality of its signalling system was crucial.' A factor of St Helena's suitability as a proper haven for the exile of Napoleon was expressed by a former governor: 'Telegraphs are placed upon the principal heights, and so spread that no vessel can approach without being descried at the distance of sixty miles. Signals from these posts are made with flags by day and lights by night, and in some cases by the firing of guns.'

Towards the end of the nineteenth century, the island's pioneering role had been forgotten, the earlier system being superseded in 1866 when the first Electric Telegraph was laid, demonstrating that the island's internal communications were keeping pace with the rest of the world.

CHAPTER 19

Blazing Ships and Treasure Wrecks

There are many wrecks in the coastal environs of St Helena, their fate ranging from the effects of battle, conflagration and scuttling.

In 1613, the Dutch EIC ship *Witte Leeuw* (White Lion) was sunk during a naval action against Portuguese vessels. In a party of four ships returning laden from Java, calling at St Helena for supplies, her cargo included nutmeg, cloves, diamonds and Chinese Ming porcelain. The wreck was found in 1976 when much of the porcelain was recovered and returned to Amsterdam. A later expedition recovered a bronze cannon now on display in the Museum of St Helena. In memory of the ship, a locally produced rum is named White Lion.

In August 1911, the New Zealand Company steamer *Papanui* embarked emigrants in London and sailed for Australia via the Canary Islands and the Cape. In early September, what became a recurring fire broke out in the coal bunkers, the escalation of which eventually led to the ship putting in at St Helena, sharing the anchorage in James Bay with the Eastern Telegraph Company cable ship *Britannia*. Staff from both ships continued to tackle the fire, but an explosion below decks made abandonment imperative. All 364 passengers and the crew of more than 100 were evacuated to shore.

The ship was entirely engulfed by the blaze, the dense clouds of smoke and flames creating a spectacle never before seen in the harbour. The ship's sides glowed red hot, and at night-time, the conflagration lit up the town. *Papanui* became a total loss and eventually settled on the bottom. The only evidence of the ship visible above water today is part of the steering gear capping the rudder and stern post. The wreck is one of the most popular dives on the island.

The passengers and crew were stranded on St Helena for some five weeks, being accommodated in the barracks, hospital and private homes. Presented with money and gifts by the islanders, they were eventually collected by the *Opawa* that completed the journey to Australia. In recognition of the kindness and hospitality extended to them, they subscribed for a bronze plaque that is exhibited outside Jamestown's Public Library.

In 1920, the Norwegian steel-hulled three-masted barque *Spangereid* appeared off Jamestown with a fire in her cargo of coal. To prevent fire from spreading aft, the captain had her towed into the beach stern first. Holing the ship at the bow to swamp her forward saved the after part of the vessel and enabled valuable property to be salvaged. On display in the dining room of the Consulate Hotel in Jamestown are artefacts that include the ship's wheel showing her original name *Fairport*, a large wooden pulley block and part of a mast.

The ship itself, with coal aboard, was offered for sale by public auction, and a wide range of goods and equipment were purchased. The captain's boat was rebuilt and was still in use in recent years as Boat 15, having previously served as harbour launch for a prolonged period. Also for many years, soft coal was sold at £1 per ton and used to fuel the suction gas engines of the island's flax mills. Originally designed for anthracite, these engines were modified for soft coal to utilise the providential supply of cheap fuel.

The former *Fairport* achieved public status during the First World War, when she unwittingly sailed between the opposing fleets at the Battle of the Falkland Islands. *Spangereid* was eventually scuttled.

In the Second World War, the predations of German submarines around St Helena sank two notable British vessels that have left enduring marks in the island's collective memory.

In 2001, on the St Helena Cenotaph that overlooks James Bay, the Darkdale Memorial Plaque was unveiled: 'Dedicated to the memory of those who were lost when RFA *Darkdale* was torpedoed and sunk in the early hours of 22 October 1941 whilst at anchor off St Helena and who have no grave but the sea.'

Forty-one seamen lost their lives when the Royal Fleet Auxiliary tanker was sunk in James Bay by the German submarine U-68, reportedly making it the first British ship sunk in the southern hemisphere during the war. The vessel was originally called *Empire Oil* before being acquired by the Admiralty in 1940, renamed and fitted with defensive weapons. *Darkdale* had been stationed at St Helena since the preceding August.

A post-war edition of *St Helena Magazine* recapped events:

a terrific explosion awoke the residents of Jamestown, five minutes later there came another explosion. The natural reaction was that an enemy raider was shelling the island.

True to the island's tradition the local inhabitants made for the wharf, not for the roads leading out of town, by which time the whole place was lit up and the Darkdale was seen ablaze from stem to stern. Indeed the whole anchorage seemed to be on fire from flaming wreckage and oil fuel.

No boats could venture near that inferno but a few of the island's boatmen stood off in hope of picking up survivors of whom only two were rescued. Such a tragedy was without parallel in living memory and everyone hung about in stunned silence.

Great was the speculation as to the cause of the disaster – was it due to a torpedo; was it due to a flash in the high octane fuel which the ship had on board? No more tankers were based at St Helena, and the island was only used for refuelling.

Only nine of the ship's complement survived. The wreck lay in shallow water with the bow extending above the surface. A hazard to shipping, a naval sloop arrived to level the wreck and determine the cause of *Darkdale*'s loss.

In 2012, the Royal Navy Ice Patrol ship HMS *Protector* visited St Helena to conduct hydrographic and environmental surveys in the vicinity of the wreck. Oil has been seeping from it since the time of sinking. In 2015, official funding was announced for the salvage of the 5,000 cubic metres of oil remaining, to protect the marine environment from potentially immeasurable damage in the event that the tanks rupture. The contractor's vessels *Pacific*

Dolphin and *Pacific Supporter* successfully carried out this operation. The last of the oil was removed to the tanker *Golden Oak*. As a final act of remembrance, the Ministry of Defence dive team attached an RFA Ensign to the wreck.

The same submarine that had attacked *Darkdale* went on to sink the British passenger ship SS *City of Cairo* the following year. On passage from Bombay to England, part of her cargo comprised 100 tons of silver coins housed in 2,000 boxes. Some 500 miles from St Helena, the U-boat's first torpedo crippled the ship. The submarine commander waited for twenty minutes, allowing the passengers and crew to evacuate into the lifeboats, before proceeding to sink her with further torpedoes. The U-boat commander's following actions have become famous. He approached the survivors and provided them with navigational information, but harboured thoughts that they would probably perish, given the remoteness of their location. On departure from the scene, in perfect English, he apologised to the survivors: 'Goodnight, sorry for sinking you.'

All but six of the 300 passengers and crew escaped to the boats. The individual fates and fortunes of each lifeboat brought both tragedy and triumph, and with considerable loss of life. A decision was made for the six boats to make for St Helena. Among so many factors for survival, in this case, the accuracy of navigation was vital. The boats became separated in bad weather. One was eventually picked up by a German ship; another found off the coast of South America with only two survivors; and the British merchantman *Bendoran* rescued forty-seven. Two other boats were picked up by SS *Clan Alpine*, within fifty miles of St Helena; a feat of navigation attributed to *City of Cairo's* second officer.

En route from Cape Town to St Helena with mail and cargo, *Clan Alpine* landed the survivors. All were accommodated, most under the care of the Salvation Army while others lived with families. The former ship's surgeon recalled: 'I had the finest meal I have ever had in my life. It was a boiled egg with bread and butter and large cupfuls of beautiful hot tea.'

Those suffering from exposure and malnutrition were restored to health in the civil and military hospitals. Despite the difficulties of housing and catering for such an unprecedented number, the islanders' renowned kindness and hospitality were pivotal in alleviating sufferings. Appreciation was evidenced before repatriations by the presentation of a fine wireless radio to the hospital. One lady married and stayed on St Helena.

In 1984, seventeen survivors met the commander of U-68 at a reunion on HMS *Belfast*, in the Pool of London, on which occasion an overheard comment was 'we couldn't have been sunk by a nicer man.'

In 2013, a British-led team broke the world underwater salvage record after recovering over £30 million worth of silver coins from the wreck of *City of Cairo*, which lies in 17,000 feet of water. A memorial plaque was left on the seabed, inscribed: 'We came here with respect.' Seven coins were presented to St Helena Museum.

In the 1990s, a deep-sea stern trawler – *Frontier* – sought help at St Helena for a vital repair. The vessel was found to be carrying illegal drugs with a value reckoned in millions of pounds. Seized and with the crew subjected to justice, the vessel was later scuttled. *Frontier* is one of four craft scuttled off Jamestown in recent years, all of which are Protected Wrecks and havens for spectacular marine life.

St Helena has a proud history of being a haven for distressed seafarers in the South Atlantic, and its inhabitants always unstinting in their humanitarian assistance to those who reach the island. In the mid-nineteenth century, survivors from the burning ship *Pole Star,* and later, *Cospatrick,* landed in a destitute state. In the 1880s, the crew of the Austrian barque *Aurora I,* which arrived on fire, accepted island hospitality. Some survivors from *Frank N Thayer,* which caught fire 700 miles from St Helena, managed to reach the island in an open boat.

In 1991, some 500 miles east of St Helena, the Saudi Arabian oil tanker ABT *Summer* was subjected to explosion and fire while en route from the Gulf to Rotterdam. Fully laden with 260,000 tons of heavy crude oil, the subsequent spill is recorded as one of the world's ten largest. Most of the slick broke up in high seas with little environmental impact. The tanker sank after three days, and five crew members perished from the incident.

A coordinated rescue response included the attendance of the refrigerated ship *Amer Himalaya* on northbound passage to Britain. Of the total of twenty-seven survivors, *Himalaya* delivered the nineteen she had rescued to St Helena. Here, those with first- and second-degree burns were treated. Testament to the level of care administered to the survivors came later from the president of Arabian Bulk Trade, writing to the island's governor, expressing on behalf of the ship's owners: 'our utmost appreciation for the assistance and cooperation you have extended to our crew, and for all you have exerted and provided to facilitate their stay and eventual repatriation, who during these periods were still in a state of distress and shock ... Your humanitarian gestures and invaluable assistance made it easier for our crew to cope with their traumatic experience.'

CHAPTER 20

Sails at Sunset and Sunrise

The golden age of sail for St Helena was the period that saw many East Indiamen a year call at the island on cargo-laden homeward-bound voyages. The ascendency of steam power, and eventually, the changing routes for trade brought the sunset of this era that has been replaced in more modern times by a rise in sail of different character and purpose.

St Helena was to be a choice port of call for the first man who sailed around the world alone – Captain Joshua Slocum. A native of Nova Scotia, he began his epic voyage at Boston, Massachusetts in 1895, having built a near-replica of a 37-foot antique oyster boat called *Spray* for the purpose. More than three years were to pass before Slocum fulfilled the prophecy of a supporter who predicted 'the *Spray* will return'.

The voyage of 46,000 miles was made entirely by sail and entirely alone. Unlike modern exponents of such cruising, or races – who are often aided by cutting-edge technologies and support in every facet of the undertaking – it was noted that Slocum had gone without power, radio, money, advertising sponsor, insurance or hospitalisation.

Three months prior to *Spray's* return home, on leaving Cape Town for the long haul in Atlantic waters, her skipper records:

> the *Spray* sailed from South Africa, the land of distances and pure air, where she had spent a pleasant and profitable time. The steam-tug *Tigre* towed her to sea from her wonted berth at the Alfred Docks, giving her a good offing. The light morning breeze, which scantily filled her sails when the tug let go the tow-line, soon died away altogether, and left her riding over a heavy swell, in full view of Table Mountain and the high peaks of the Cape of Good Hope.

The following day a breeze came, and 'the *Spray* soon sailed the highest peaks of the mountains out of sight, and the world changed from a mere panoramic view to the light of a homeward-bound voyage.' As with the East Indiamen of old, the south-east trade wind suited *Spray* and made for excellent sailing:

> And so the *Spray* reeled off the miles, showing a good run every day till April 11, which came almost before I knew it. Very early that morning I was awakened by that rare bird,

the booby, with its harsh quack, which I recognized at once as a call to go on deck; it was as much as to say 'Skipper, there's land in sight.' I tumbled out quickly, and sure enough, away ahead in the dim twilight, about twenty miles off, was St Helena.

My first impulse was to call out, 'Oh, what a speck in the sea!' It is in reality nine miles in length and two thousand eight hundred and twenty-three feet in height.

On landing, Slocum went to pay his respects to the governor, Sir R. Sterndale, who remarked that it was not often, in those days, that a circumnavigator came via St Helena. He issued a cordial invitation for the adventurer to tell of his voyage, first at Garden Hall to the local people and then at Plantation House, the governor's residence, to both himself and the officers of the garrison and their friends. Slocum recalled: 'I remained at Plantation House a couple of days, and one of the rooms in the mansion, called the "west room", being haunted, the butler, by command of his Excellency, put me up in that – like a prince.'

The governor treated the visitor to a tour of the island by carriage. He was most impressed:

At one point of our journey the road, in winding around spurs and ravines, formed a perfect W within the distance of a few rods. The roads, though tortuous and steep, were fairly good, and I was struck with the amount of labour it must have cost to build them. It is said that, since hanging for trivial offenses went out of fashion, no one has died there, except from falling over the cliffs in old age, or from being crushed by stones rolling on them from the steep mountains!

On 20 April, *Spray* was ready for sea. The governor's wife presented Slocum with a large fruit cake to be taken on the voyage, and mail was assembled for delivery to Ascension. He records his departure:

It was late in the evening before the anchor was up, and I bore off for the west, loath to leave my new friends. But fresh winds filled the sloop's sails once more, and I watched the beacon-light at Plantation House, the governor's parting signal for the *Spray,* till the island faded in the darkness astern and became one with the night, and by midnight the light itself had disappeared below the horizon.

Aboard *Spray* was an unusual 'gift' from St Helena; one that her skipper could have done without. An American on the island 'in an evil moment, had put a goat on board'. The animal was intended to have been useful and as companionable as a dog. In reality, it turned out to be 'the worst pirate I met on the whole voyage'. Its depredations began by consuming the chart of the West Indies – the want of which later led almost to shipwreck and caused Slocum to record: 'I could have nailed the St Helena goat's pelt to the deck.' There was not a tethering rope onboard proof against its teeth, to which the sea-jacket and shore-going straw hat succumbed. Ascension Island could not be reached soon enough to land the creature ashore.

Simon's Town is an historical naval village not far from Cape Town. It is home to both the South African Navy and the False Bay Yacht Club. The year 1996 saw the inauguration of a biennial sailing event known as the Governor's Cup Yacht Race. Organised by the club at False Bay, it is a 1,700 mile downwind ocean passage starting at Simon's Town and finishing at Jamestown, St Helena. The race, which begins in December, has been promoted abroad as 'The Ultimate Christmas Getaway' and is claimed to be on many yachtsmen's 'bucket list' of desirable things to do.

The 2012 race was won by *Banjo,* crossing the line on New Year's Day. Her skipper spoke on St Helena Radio: 'It was absolutely beautiful approaching the island at this time of evening, the sun was behind the island, it looked fantastic.' Part and parcel of the many unusual consignments for carriage aboard RMS *St Helena* were yachts participating in the race, which were transported as deck cargo back to Cape Town.

In the same month, St Helena was visited by participants in the World ARC Rally, an international 'round the world' sailing expedition starting at St Lucia in the Caribbean, which was also the finishing point. St Helena's newspaper headlines broadcast: '22 yachts due in, starting this week' and quoted a visitor's response: 'the fleet were so delighted by the welcome they got from Saints as they walked in the street, visited the pub or spent money in the shops. We found St Helena to be one of the friendliest places we visited.'

Sailing vessels of grand stature are also keen to visit St Helena. The Norwegian tall ship *Sørlandet,* which was built in 1927 as a school ship for training young people for a career in the home country's merchant fleet, called at the island in 2013. Chartered by the Canadian-based West Island College for their Class Afloat programme, it offered an ocean-going high school cum university experience for one term to a full year, with the bonus of visiting a mix of exotic destinations. This particular season began in Istanbul. Subsequent calls included Rhodes, Dubrovnik, Corsica, Lisbon, Agadir, Fernando da Noronha, Natal, Rio de Janeiro, Cape Town and Walvis Bay in Namibia. After leaving St Helena, *Sørlandet* called at Ascension, eventually finishing at Lunenburg, Canada.

It was with the noble aim of promoting a reclaimed culture that the sailing Hawaiian voyaging canoe *Hokule'a* moored up in James Bay, St Helena in 2016, having travelled from Walvis Bay. Her crew had an environmental message to spread to small islands: to encourage a greater sense of island community worldwide. *Hokule'a*'s first journey in the 1970s was a groundbreaking scientific experiment that showed – long before DNA evidence – the Asiatic origin of Polynesian people. This initial voyage helped resurrect the ailing culture of Hawaii.

The canoe's recent visit to St Helena, at a time when the island was on the brink of 'going global' due to the imminent completion of its international airport, was a timely recognition and reminder of the shared values to be found and celebrated within all remote island communities around the world.

CHAPTER 21

The Union-Castle Connection

Union-Castle Line was one of Britain's great shipping companies. Its origins were in the Union Line established in 1855 and Castle Line that began trading in 1862. The two companies merged in 1900. The developed passenger liner and cargo services from Britain provided a double halo of routes that circled the continent of Africa and regularly touched the remote and romantic islands of St Helena and Ascension. The elegance of the mail ships, dubbed in the local idiom as 'Cape Boats', was enhanced by the distinctive French Grey lavender colour of their hulls, while the punctuality of their scheduled departures from Britain became a byword by which it was capable to set clocks.

*

In 1857, the Union Steam Ship Company successfully tendered for a mail service between England and Cape Town in South Africa. A monthly service was to be maintained in each direction, and it was inaugurated by the small steamer *Dane*. At the time, her crew and six passengers were unaware of making history, as the forerunners of the magnificent service that was to come. St Helena, too, became involved at an early stage. In 1858, Union Line ships commenced homeward-bound calls for mails at St Helena and Ascension.

In 1862, Castle Line was founded, its sailing ships plying between Liverpool and Calcutta. These vessels were given the names of castles, names that were to be perpetuated beyond the mid-twentieth century. In 1876, the Castle Mail Packets Company came into being, coincident with the expiry of the mail contract held by Union Line. The new contract was divided between the two companies that were able to provide a weekly mail service to the Cape colony. For twenty-five years, there was intense competition between the companies that provided the service on alternate weeks. Each strove to provide bigger, better and faster ships, before the companies finally merged.

*

In the early 1950s, Harland & Wolff of Belfast built three new *Castles*. These operated the 'Round Africa' service together with three pre-existing *Castles*. Three circumnavigated Africa in each direction. From London, via the Suez Canal, the itinerary was Gibraltar, Marseilles, Genoa, Port Said, Port Sudan, Aden, Mombasa, Tonga, Zanzibar, Dar es Salaam, Beira, Lourenco Marques, Durban, East London, Port Elizabeth, Cape Town, St Helena, Ascension, Las Palmas. Outwards, via the West Coast was in reverse.

As international airline services developed in the 1950s, a downward trend in sea travel on passenger ships began, a process that initiated downsizing the numbers of ships and services. Union-Castle made strategic fleet-wide changes. An innovation was the building of two sister-ship cargo liners – the first cargo-only vessels built for the mail service. Their powerful engines enabled them to maintain their places in the schedules and became known as 'mini mails'. *Southampton Castle* was the first of the new ships, launched in October 1964 and followed four months later by *Good Hope Castle*. They were later fitted with twelve passenger berths, an alteration underwritten by the British government, as they alone called at Ascension Island and St Helena. Deck passengers were also carried on the inter-island route.

These two ships were the fastest diesel-powered cargo liners afloat, designed for a service speed of 22.5 knots, but capable of more. The hull form incorporated a cruiser stern and raked stem with bulbous bow. The single extremely large funnel, which appeared to overwhelm the superstructure, housed two waste heat boilers used to supply steam for a turbo-alternator providing electrical power while on passage.

Deadweight exceeded 11,000 tons with large capacities for deciduous and citrus fruits. With temperature control, a wide range of frozen products could also be carried. There were four holds forward, and three aft served by an impressive suite of derricks. Several of the hatches were capable of carrying containers. Wine could also be carried in bulk, with thirteen permanent tanks and associated piping to handle 60,000 gallons.

The delivery of *Good Hope Castle* was delayed by labour shortages at the builders and was taken into service four months behind schedule, her place being temporarily filled by *Capetown Castle*. This ship retained the distinction of being not only the largest motor-driven liner in the company, but also the longest of her type in the world. When this ship was relieved by *Good Hope Castle,* she was refitted and continued for two years in a 'one class' extra service calling sometimes at Ascension, St Helena and Walvis Bay, Namibia.

The disposal of Union-Castle ships continued and was to mark the demise of its passenger trade to the East Africa coast. Practically, all colonies of the British Empire had reached independence, with the consequent rundown of their colonial officers, administrators and civil servants who had helped to fill the passenger lists. Those that remained were now using the ever-expanding air services.

On 1 July 1973, St Helena reported that *Good Hope Castle,* which should have arrived there the previous evening, had been in radio silence since leaving Ascension. Neither could she be raised on the radio by her sister-ship. Fears were confirmed in a later message from Ascension. A machinery-space fire had spread to the accommodation; the ship was ablaze and had been abandoned, burning and listing, but that everyone was safe. The eighty-two passengers and crew spent some 36 hours in lifeboats before being taken aboard the Liberian tanker *George F. Getty* and landed at Ascension.

The stricken ship was attended by the West German ocean salvage tug *Albatros* that towed the vessel to Antwerp. Another Bugsier tug, *Heros*, took the ship to Bilbao. After extensive repairs, *Good Hope Castle* resumed service in May 1974.

Officially, the Southampton to South Africa mail service ended with the arrival of *Southampton Castle* on 24 October 1977, over 120 years after the inauguration. The two fast cargo liners were sold to an Italian company. They traded for a further six years between Italy and South America. The very last call at St Helena was made by the northbound *Windsor Castle.*

In keeping with St Helena's status in maritime heritage and worldwide interest in its postage stamps, the island celebrated the role of *Good Hope Castle* on an 80p stamp.

In the wake of Union-Castle, with a subsidy from the British government to continue a service to St Helena and Ascension, the St Helenian government and Curnow Shipping established the St Helena Shipping company, thereby opening a whole new and significant chapter in providing a maritime connection for these South Atlantic islands.

CHAPTER 22

The Ship Formerly Known as *Prince*

When Union-Castle relinquished its shipping interests, and the mail contract was awarded to the small Cornwall-based British management company of Curnow Shipping, they advantageously obtained a suitable vessel to begin the service. Called *Northland Prince,* she was operated until 1976 by Northland Navigation of Canada, carrying passengers and freight between Vancouver and the Queen Charlotte Islands via Prince Rupert. A little over 3,000 gross tons, she made the Atlantic crossing to Britain and was refitted in Southampton. Now capable of carrying seventy-six passengers on international voyages and officially renamed *St Helena* by HRH Princess Margaret, she was based at the port of Avonmouth, near Bristol.

Partly staffed with officers previously with Union-Castle Line, the crew were recruited from St Helena, and they were to prove ideal. The first port of call on leaving Britain was at Las Palmas, Gran Canaria, essentially to take on fuel and fresh stores for the week-long passage to Ascension Island.

At Ascension, the ship was able to embark a further forty-eight, as deck passengers for St Helena. These were workers returning home on leave, St Helena then being the mainstay for the workforce. Principal employers were the BBC, Cable & Wireless, NASA and the air base at Wideawake. The passage of some 700 miles took two days during which the deck passengers were given exclusive use of the stern gallery lounge, but had to sleep using the boat deck as a dormitory that had laced canvas screens rigged for the purpose. A radio officer who had served on *Good Hope Castle* recalled how deck passengers were easily absorbed because of that ship's size. On the relatively small *St Helena*, there was always relief on arriving at the St Helena anchorage where the noisy but happy crowd were able to disembark.

All passengers otherwise generally had the run of the ship. In warmer settled climes, the foredeck was used for deck sports such as cricket, tug of wars, wheelbarrow and egg-and-spoon races, as well as other activities appropriate to the available space. A swimming pool that was formerly a storage tank was jury-rigged and filled each day.

Southbound voyages incorporated a shuttle run from St Helena back to Ascension to facilitate workers returning to work. The remainder of the voyage south from St Helena terminated at Cape Town. Northbound voyages were originally shorter, as the ship continued her passage from Ascension towards the Canary Islands. After several voyages, the port of call here was changed to Santa Cruz, Tenerife.

The islands of St Helena, Ascension and Tristan da Cunha further to the south all share the quality of being coveted and acquired for national strategic purposes. In the early 1980s, the Falkland Islands became the focus of such attentions. In the conflict with Argentina that was to follow, St Helena was to feel some of the ripples it generated.

St Helena departed as normal from Avonmouth at the start of Voyage 25. During her progress south, the Falklands were invaded by Argentina, after which a British Task Force was dispatched. This force, comprising numerous warships and merchant vessels, arrived at Ascension ahead of *St Helena.* As she began working cargo, her presence was noted by a senior officer from HMS *Invincible* who initiated an inspection of the ship that led to speculation that *St Helena* could be requisitioned.

On the ship's eventual northbound call at Tenerife, naval officers again boarded to assess her suitability as a support ship. After resuming the voyage, it was confirmed that she would be taken into naval service on arrival at Avonmouth. Undergoing an extensive refit at Portsmouth Dockyard, *St Helena*'s role was to support and enable independent operations by two mine-hunters, HMS *Brecon* and HMS *Ledbury.* Equipped with a Wasp helicopter and anti-aircraft armaments, she was fitted with the means to carry out Replenishment at Sea.

The group sailed from Portland in mid-June 1982. Only volunteers from the officers and crew manned the ship. As the latter resided on St Helena, this was the only means of getting home. Many operational exercises were carried out during the voyage. Sailing under strict radio silence, in reality, the Argentinean surrender took place the day after her departure from Portland, but as the flotilla was not a fighting unit, their main operational function was to be mine clearance while the main Task Force were kept in full readiness. By the end of July, most of the group's work had been completed, and they sailed for the UK a fortnight later. An impromptu call at St Helena enabled some crew to go on leave and prompted a formal reception and cocktail party for the officers and senior naval ratings.

Throughout the further passage, regular refuelling and transfer of stores by helicopter took place. After a brief period of rest and recuperation at Gibraltar, the flotilla finally berthed at Rosyth Dockyard in Scotland, home base for the two mine-hunters. The Royal Navy acknowledged that the three small ships had made a noteworthy contribution by operating independently and efficiently so far from home.

St Helena sailed to a repair yard in North East England for essential repairs before taking on service as a troop transport and store ship in the Falklands, with a schedule to operate between Ascension, Port Stanley and Grytviken in South Georgia. Here, she made a number of shuttle visits to relieve the recently established British garrison.

Following a final call at the Falklands, *St Helena* returned to Britain and was reconverted at the repair yard in Falmouth, bringing this singular year-long charter to a close. While the ship remained temporarily in lay-up with a skeleton crew, HRH Princess Margaret paid a return visit as part of the 150th anniversary celebrations of St Helena being a Crown colony.

Once more back in service, *St Helena* was to suffer a near-fatal incident. Off the coast of West Africa, she suffered a serious engine-room fire. In tackling it, the ship consequently developed a list. Two vessels answered the distress call, one of which, the tanker *Overseas*

Argonaut, provided substantial comfort by her presence on scene. Eventually, the German salvage tug *Fairplay IX* towed the ship to Dakar for repair.

In 1987, following a decision by the British government to replace the ageing *St Helena* with a purpose-built new vessel, a contract was awarded to a British shipbuilder. As the new ship was also to be called *St Helena,* the original was renamed *St Helena Island.* She was to see service offering cruises in the Seychelles under new owners, as *Avalon.* The venture was short-lived and after a final flurry of activity, this remarkable little vessel was deconstructed in India.

In the guise for which she is most remembered, *St Helena* was colourfully celebrated on a 20p St Helena stamp. In the foyer of her replacement, a splendid scratch-built model built by long-serving radio officer Robert Wilson was regularly admired.

In 2014, the St Helena government announced that the volunteer crew of RMS *St Helena,* who sailed to the Falklands during the conflict, were eligible to apply for the South Atlantic Medal: a deserving recognition.

CHAPTER 23

A Replacement Bus Service

The requisitioning of *St Helena* by the Royal Navy left a need for stopgap arrangements to be made to maintain maritime links for St Helena. In the first instance, this was quickly filled by *Lady Roslin,* a small vessel built in 1958 for ICI in Scotland, to transport explosives. Refitted to carry twelve passengers, she began service for St Helena under the name *Aragonite,* plying between Cape Town, St Helena and Ascension.

Although proving successful, *Aragonite* was not substantial enough for the service, prompting a charter with Straits Shipping Company – a subsidiary of Blue Funnel Line – for the passenger-cargo liner *Centaur* that occupied the Hong Kong–Australia route: a vessel with a capacity for nearly 200 passengers, and general cargo capacity was able to transport several thousand live sheep. Consideration was also given to using *Centaur* as a permanent replacement for *St Helena,* but was later deemed not entirely suitable. Completing her charter, she resumed her former operations in the East.

CHAPTER 24

A Miscellany of Visitors

The Confidence of Captain Cook

Captain James Cook briefly paused at St Helena on the return leg of both his first and second world voyages. On both occasions, he approached the island from the Cape of Good Hope. The first time, he followed the common practice of aiming for a point well to the east and then, on the certainty of reaching the island's latitude, steered west until land was sighted. On the second voyage, Cook resolved to make the island by a direct course. Accompanied by an East Indiaman, that ship expressed concern that they would miss the island. Captain Cook is recorded as having laughed, advising them that 'he would run their jib-boom on the Island if they choose'.

An Appreciative Visit by Captain Bligh

In December 1792, Captain Bligh – hero of the *Bounty* – arrived at St Helena on the return from his second voyage to the South Seas. His ships, *Providence* and *Assistant,* were laden with breadfruit trees for Jamaica.

Of his coming to St Helena, Bligh records:

At noon after I anchored, an officer was sent from the Governor, Lt-Colonel Brooke, to welcome us. I landed at 1 o'clock when I was saluted with 13 guns, and the Governor received me. In my interview with him, I informed him of my orders to give into his care 10 breadfruit plants, and one of every kind (of which I had five), as would secure to the island a lasting supply of this valuable fruit which our most gracious King had ordered to be planted there. Colonel Brooke expressed great gratitude and the principal plants were taken to a valley near his residence called Plantation House, and the rest to James Valley ... I also left a quantity of mountain rice seed here. The sago was the only plant that required a particular description. I therefore took our Otahetian friends to the Governor's House where they made a pudding of the prepared part of its root, some of which I had brought from Otaheite.

Bligh observed of the island:

> Few places look more unhealthy when sailing along its burnt-up cliffs – huge masses of rock fit only to resist the sea, yet few places are more healthy. The inhabitants are not like other Europeans who live in the Torrid Zone, but have good constitutions – the women being fair and pretty. James Town, the capital, lies in a deep and narrow valley, and it is little more than one long street of houses; these are built after our English fashion, most of them having thatched roofs. Lodgings are scarce, so I was fortunate in finding rooms with Captain Statham in a well-regulated house at the common rate of twelve shillings a day. The Otahetians were delighted with what they saw here, as Colonel Brooke showed them kind attention, had them stay at his house, and gave them each a suit of red clothes.

Before Captain Bligh left the island, a letter was despatched to him from the governor and council, in which thanks were conveyed for the gifts, declaring that they 'had impressed their minds with the warmest gratitude towards His Majesty for his goodness and attention for the welfare of his subjects; while the sight of his ships had raised in them an inexpressible degree of wonder and delight to contemplate a floating garden transported in luxuriance from one extremity of the world to the other.'

The 'Infamous' William Hickey

The Englishman William Hickey, described as having 'made up for an ill-spent life by leaving behind him one of the most entertaining books of memoirs in the English language' stayed on St Helena for eight days in 1793, during a voyage from Calcutta to England on *Eden Castle*. The stormy voyage allowed him and his fellow travellers to be delighted when 'At noon we had the gratification of seeing the land from the deck, and never did I feel more pleasure than in beholding that little speck in the midst of an immense ocean.'

On leaving the island, Hickey observed: 'St. Helena is much more beautiful and picturesque in sailing from it than in approaching towards it, as in departing you have in view the rich and fertile valley with a remarkably neat and handsome town as well as a variety of country houses and gardens in different directions, forming an interesting and agreeable appearance of verdure or capacity of cultivation.'

A Child's Recollection of Napoleon

The famous English novelist William Thackeray was six years of age when he visited St Helena in 1817 during a passage from India to England. While on the island, he sighted Napoleon, an incident to which he made later reference as an essayist in a column known as *Roundabout Papers*. Recalling the childhood incident, he remembered being told that Napoleon 'eats three sheep every day, and all the little children he can lay hands on!'

A Millennium Stowaway Considers Political Asylum

In 2000, a teenage boy from Burundi stowed away on the RMS *St Helena* while the vessel was docked in Cape Town. He was discovered shortly before the ship arrived at St Helena. He related tales of atrocities endured by himself and his family. Passengers held a collection, and it was suggested that the young man apply for political asylum on the island.

He was warmly received and given support by government officials. The youth eventually decided to withdraw his application for asylum. The factor that had decided him to stowaway was the name 'London' on the stern. He had wrongly concluded that the ship was bound for the UK. He was surprised and disappointed when the ship arrived at St Helena. He ultimately achieved his aim, eventually being transported to Britain.

French Warships: Entente Cordiale

In April 2014, St Helena hosted a visit of two major French warships: the Force Projection and Command Ship FS *Mistral* and the advanced frigate FS *La Fayette*. In a programme organised by the honorary French Consul, he acknowledged that 'The call of the two main vessels of the Groupe Jeanne d'Arc is quite an honour ... St Helena owns a great page of our common history and this port of call further honours our mutual respect.' The ships then travelled to South America to provide help in the prevention of drug smuggling. The visit was later described as a successful Naval Charm Assault on St Helena.

All Fuelled Up

St Helena's fuel stocks are supplied by periodic visits by tankers that anchor and moor in Rupert's Bay, for pumping ashore via floating pipeline. The *Jo Acer* regularly carries out these deliveries, which occur every few months. In May 2012, 686 tons of diesel fuel and 150 tons of petrol were delivered. In late 2015, 'Good Old Jo' – the *Jo Larix* – arrived with fuel. The ship's crew were greeted with the unusual sight of Rupert's Wharf under construction and protruding proudly into the bay.

The current arrangement supersedes an earlier operation carried out by a former British coastal tanker. Built in 1961 as *Esso Dover,* the vessel was acquired in 1980 from Cherry Marine, under the name *Cherrybobs*. Obtained by St Helena Shipping and renamed *Bosun Bird*, the tanker brought fuel from Ascension for St Helena. Here, she lay at anchor as a floating fuel store, her oil not only used for domestic purposes, but also for the RMS *St Helena*. Until then, oil had been imported in drums from South Africa, as there was limited demand for it on the island.

Helping Hands Across the Seas

The front-page newspaper headline of St Helena's *Sentinel* was eye-catching: 'EVACUATED IN THE DEAD OF NIGHT! – Dutch Ship Rushes to Rescue Sick Child'. A seven-year-old girl,

Abbe, was in acute need of off-island medical attention, but RMS *St Helena* was several days' distant. In the UK, HM's Coast Guard in Falmouth received a call from St Helena Hospital for assistance in arranging a medical evacuation. They responded by calling Search and Rescue organisations around the world and making satellite broadcasts on behalf of St Helena Radio.

The Dutch container ship MV *Traveller,* on passage from South Africa to the British Virgin Islands, responded to a Mayday from the island. Owned by the company BigLift, the ship was praised for its unstinting assistance, which included funding the costs of the operation. The girl arrived in a stable condition at Ascension where an air ambulance was waiting. The following day, she was admitted to Great Ormond Street Hospital in London. The same newspaper happily reported later from Abbe's mother:

> Abbe is doing much better, it's nice to hear her laughing. She still gets very tired but that is part of the recovery. We have been in the UK for almost two weeks and yet it feels much longer. I am very grateful to the community of St Helena and Ascension, who have supported us at this very difficult time, please know that I receive all your messages on Facebook and I am so amazed at how everyone's prayers are with us. Thank you so much.

Just Passing

In February 2016, people on the north side of St Helena were surprised to observe out to sea a huge alien-looking structure come slowly into view, preceded by a more conventional and recognisable craft. The combination turned out to be a tug and tow. Leading the slow procession was the red-hulled *Skandi Admiral,* a Norwegian anchor-handling tug and supply vessel. Her charge, which at first sight resembled some form of drilling rig, was actually the Pipe Layer Platform *Castoro 7.* Designed for specialist operations associated with the oil and gas industries, its other-worldly appearance and looming presence off Jamestown would have stimulated the imaginations, especially of devotees of *Star Wars,* its battle-scarred and rusting structure adding to the mystery. This 180-m giant sprouted unlikely and unexplained appendages extending at all angles from its high main platform. The filigree latticed jibs of cranes were the only recognisable elements.

The forty-year-old platform was reportedly being taken from the Caribbean to South Africa, to be scrapped. In time-honoured fashion, St Helena was once again used as a provision store, this time in a drive-by capacity. Having earlier contacted an agent on the island with orders for restocking the ship, the tug and tow slowed to some two knots, allowing the island launch *Gannet Three* to make a convenient rendezvous.

Some days prior to this, and with the uncanny coincidental timings so often observed in the vastness of the open oceans, RMS *St Helena* passed the *Castoro 7* while heading to Ascension Island and again on her return, in the environs of St Helena.

Bring Out Your Antiques

Viewers of television programmes about antiques will recognise the name Tim Wonnacott. A regular participant and presenter, he is a British celebrity and an expert on the subject.

In April 2016, Mr Wonnacott and his wife made a return visit to St Helena on the RMS; this time to carry out valuations of local antiques on the island, in the style of an Antiques Roadshow. Planned as a two-hour event at the Grand Parade, such was its popularity that the Bargain Hunt star stayed all day. He viewed stamps, pictures, paintings, coins, statues, heirlooms and furniture. Most items were not found to be valuable, although some were valued beyond their owners' expectations.

The Rovers' Return

In May 2013, the Small Fleet Tanker *Black Rover,* which supports the ships of the Royal Navy, made an official visit to St Helena, to be present for St Helena Day. The ship hosted the island's acting governor, and the crew took part in activities on the day. A quiz run by the local radio station resulted in fourteen winners, who won not only a tour of the ship but also a three-hour passage around the island, in calm and beautiful weather. Youngster Jacob Williams admitted: 'I'm enjoying the trip. Auntie Cynthia had the question right on the radio and gave the trip to me and Dad.'

In May 2016, *Gold Rover,* sister-ship to *Black Rover,* made her final scheduled visit to St Helena. She stayed for ten days, allowing the crew to explore the island and also to take part in the St Helena Day celebrations. The ship has visited the islands on many occasions and even celebrated with the islanders the 200th anniversary of Napoleon's arrival in exile, when she was in company with the frigate HMS *Lancaster.* On this occasion, in the UK, a plaque was unveiled in Plymouth to mark Napoleon's ten-day captivity in Plymouth Sound. It contains a piece of volcanic stone from Longwood House where Napoleon lived out his exile. The stone was transported by the French Navy and Brittany Ferries and is inscribed: 'May our hearts be open to friendship and our arms reach across the sea to unite our two nations.'

In 2016, the *Gold Rover* and *Black Rover* were the only Rover class vessels on duty in the world. The other three vessels of the class had already been phased out and replaced with environmentally safer double-hulled ships. After her visit, *Gold Rover* assisted with naval exercises with other ships, but will return to the UK in 2017 for decommissioning.

An Urgent Bank Withdrawal

In June 2016, a small ferry called *Don Baldo* arrived at St Helena from the Falkland Islands en route to western Africa for delivery to a new owner. This vessel, which can carry a few hundred passengers and some vehicles, paused at the island to await a money transfer from the buyer's account for the crew. After two days, the ferry continued to her destination.

CHAPTER 25

Let's Go Cruising

In April 2012, the cruise ship *Arcadia* anchored in James Bay, carrying nearly 1,900 passengers. Reportedly, it was a promising day for all local traders to 'hit the street' with their products and services. Two security officers from the ship went ashore to check sea conditions. They deemed it unsafe for landing at the Wharf steps. A local ferry operator indicated that conditions were assessed at the time of a tide change that can initiate a swell: 'They had their boat tied up in the steps for two hours and more, the boat could get easily onto the steps ... St Helena lost a lot of money today.' Evidently, the average age of the passengers was seventy-five years. The company has regulations that prohibit landing passengers if swell exceeds half a metre. The potential economic loss to the island was reckoned to be in the order of £50,000 to local businesses, and £20,000 to government revenue on landing fees.

In February 2015, the cruise ship *Voyager* made a scheduled call at St Helena. Onboard were a couple who were serving as hosts for the card game of Bridge. On the morning of the ship's arrival, the gentleman fainted in the very hot weather. Tests made by the ship's doctor found the couple being denied re-embarkation from the island, despite doctors at the General Hospital confirming the couple's family doctor's assessment of being fit to travel. *Voyager* duly sailed without the couple, forcing them to wait eighteen days before being able to leave. It was their opinion that, in any event, staying on the ship was the best option: 'If I was ill enough to require urgent treatment [the doctor] should have kept me on the *Voyager*, because the next stop was Ascension.' The operators advised that they had contacted the passenger's insurance company to apprise them of the situation and claimed to be offering as much support as possible.

It is more usual for cruise ship passengers to be thrilled with their visiting experiences, such as from *Amsterdam*. Over 900 explorers landed in perfect conditions of sea and weather. A popular challenge is the climbing of the famous incline of Jacob's Ladder, which scales the height from Main Street to the summit of Ladder Hill. A testing 699 steps, and those who succeed are eligible to receive certificates. On this day, over 100 certificates were issued from the island museum at the foot of the steps.

On the *Astor*, the majority of passengers were British, Australian and German. A Dutch admirer enthused: 'It is a lovely picturesque place. I like the streets, houses and courtyards. It is also very peaceful.' Already considering a return to the island, he admitted that he would prefer to travel by ship, as it is more exciting.

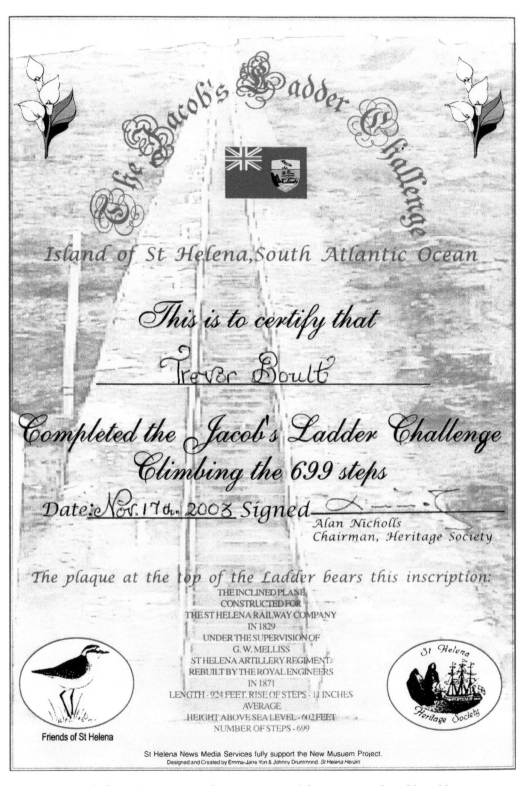

A popular challenge for visitors is the steep ascent of the 699 steps of Jacob's Ladder, Jamestown.

CHAPTER 26

Ships Make Planes Possible

In the past 500 years, innumerable maritime events have taken place at St Helena. However, such historic events are not consigned to the past. In July 2012, the very first ship 'docked' at the island – a momentous occasion that materially demonstrated how St Helena is to relinquish its celebrated status of remoteness to the wider world.

As a fundamental link in the process of constructing St Helena's first-ever airport, a facility that will provide international connections and two-way access for economic development, the ship NP *Glory 4* berthed bow-first at the temporarily ramped jetty in Rupert's Bay.

The ship is operated by Basil Read, the contractor for the construction of the airport and the associated infrastructure required for this exceptional project. Much of the heavy plant, equipment and materials were brought to the island from Walvis Bay, Namibia, by *Glory 4* that was soon affectionately referred to by the islanders as 'the Basil Read ship'. A Thai-owned vessel, she operated under a three-year charter. Some 80 m long, with a 70-ton bow ramp, she has 800 square metres of deck space with gear capable of handling 30 ton loads.

The docking of *Glory 4* at St Helena in 2012 was a double first. Historically, for the island, she was the first-ever ship to actually secure at a berth, and for Basil Read, it was a new experience to ship equipment to a project site by sea. The vessel was carefully manoeuvred using as visual guides white diamond-shaped markers and flashing amber lights secured to the cliff face of Munden's Hill. Her arrival signified the start of major construction works for the airport. Thereafter, *Glory 4* made what became routine visits to the island every three weeks, with project cargo.

On a subsequent call, a trip to see the ship by young pupils from St Paul's School brought a flurry of appreciative reporting to the island's *Sentinel* newspaper: Brooke enthused 'When we looked at the Basil Read ship it was low down in the water, because it was holding heavy containers. I felt very happy that day, because I have never seen a ship so close before.'

In April 2012, Basil Read utilised the RMS *St Helena* to carry the two largest vehicles that would fit, or be lifted by, the ship's cranes. The two Volvo articulated dump trucks weighed 24 tons, with carrying capacity of 30 tons. After the usual trans-shipping to St Helena's

Wharf, the vehicles were paired to work with excavators brought subsequently by *Glory 4*. Other heavy equipment included bulldozer, drilling rigs, crusher and concrete batching plant, and the bulk carriage of fuel for the operation of plant.

As well as the airport proper, the project also included jetty construction and upgrades to existing infrastructure, facilities for fuel storage, the creation of a 14-km haul road, temporary accommodation and support facilities for workers.

CHAPTER 27

A Fondness for Fishing

St Helena has an established fishery, traditionally supporting mainly small local craft. In 2013, the island was briefly visited by its newest licensed commercial offshore fishing boat, *Southern Cross,* operated by the South African company Global Fish. A local fisherman joined the crew for an exploratory trial of several months to assess the viability of pole and line fishing, with the catch being landed in South Africa. As the airport project was underway, having a number of these licensed and regulated vessels landing their catches at St Helena could provide lucrative export revenue. On her first trip, the 29 m *Southern Cross* caught 62 tons of yellow fin and big-eyed tuna. Local stakeholders were concerned that the waters around St Helena may be fished illegally. *Southern Cross* was then the only vessel licensed to fish in these waters. An additional mandate was to record vessels that may have been acting outside of the law.

In 2014, the fishing vessel *Extractor* completed a week-long ocean passage from Hout Bay, South Africa. Owned by Saint Marine Resources, five St Helena boats made up a welcoming flotilla. The boat's arrival was heralded in the press: 'Economic Development has started on the Island.' At the end of the following year, *Extractor* landed a record catch. Loaded for a three-week trip, she returned much earlier with the holds brim full, vindicating the opinion 'we always knew there were larger stocks out at the sea mounts': reassuring news for local operators of *Amalia* that had also recently arrived from South Africa.

As a variation, in 2014, the 42-feet multipurpose motor vessel *Enchanted Isle* arrived at St Helena, the culmination of over two years of planning. Of a design well known as a coastal patrol boat, this craft is suited for work in the waters around St Helena and was soon referred to as 'The Porsche of the Sea'. The entrepreneurial young owner–operators had an impressive business plan: 'In addition to tours already offered, like dolphin trips, whale watching and so forth, we will also be including other things like game and sports fishing.' Also night-time trips 'to take people out to look at the stars in the middle of the ocean – something that hasn't been on offer by other boat owners on the island.'

Enchanted Isle took part in a special international study of whale sharks in their natural habitat. The largest sharks in the world, tags were fixed to them that provided detailed information on behaviour when out of sight and where they go at night. The boat's crew are among a small handful of people in the world known to have witnessed whale sharks mating in the wild.

CHAPTER 28

Heralding in the New

The South African airline company Comair was chosen to provide the new service for St Helena on behalf of British Airways. The brand new Boeing 737-800 assigned to the route made the four-hour 'implementation flight' from Johannesburg on 18 April 2016. Hundreds of spectators witnessed the historic event. Before taxiing onto the apron, the pilot and co-pilot threw open the side windows and draped the flags of St Helena and South Africa down the front of the plane. The aircraft carried some fifty passengers and was heavily laden with cargo, mostly a consignment of aircraft spare parts to be kept on the island.

It was a time of mixed emotions for the islanders; saddened by the prospect of the eventual loss of RMS *St Helena*, but excited by the many opportunities arising from air travel. In 1984, a Hercules aircraft flew past the island to assess the possibilities of a runway. Its eventual fruition is intended to make St Helena more accessible to the world, and vice versa. In the words of the island's Father Dale Bowers, 'how we cope with that and how we manage that is important.'

A month after the historic first flight landed at Prosperous Bay Plain, A. W. Ship Management secured the contract to supply St Helena by sea after the airport officially opens. The vessel acquired for the purpose can carry up to four times more containers than RMS *St Helena* and will have accommodation for twelve passengers – the most allowed under international law. The ship's new name is to be MV *Helena,* the suggestion that won the most votes cast on the company's website, with runners up being *Wirebird* and *Rupert's Bay.*

July 2016 saw the historic first docking at the new facility in Rupert's Bay of MV *Greta.* She berthed stern first, port-side to the quay to enable full outreach of the ship's cranes to lift 60 ton pieces of plant.

By such careful and incremental activities, the transition of St Helena 'going global' takes due note of Father Bowers's wise counsel.

CHAPTER 29

'Last Boat to St Helena'

In the summer of 2016, the London-based rock band Everafter released a new single entitled *Last Boat to St Helena*. Inspired by the media spotlight then being directed at this extraordinary island, which was soon to be 'going global' with the anticipated opening of its international airport, a family member of the band had expressed a wish to sail on the RMS *St Helena* on her final voyage to St Helena. This in turn led to the creation of the song's lyrics and music.

Directed at a young generation, the song yet speaks to all of the significance and poignancy of the event when, at whatever time, *St Helena* makes her ultimate voyage on behalf of the island community she has so faithfully and effectively served.

St Helena was built in Aberdeen and launched by HRH Prince Andrew in 1989. She was the first purpose-built motor-ship to service the lifeline passenger, mail and general cargo needs of the island. In April 2016, the island's *Sentinel* newspaper ran an arresting headline: 'Ship for Sale: RMS Looking for New Owner.' A statement from her owners – St Helena Line – was optimistic for her future: '[the ship's] combined passenger accommodation and cargo design makes her well-suited to a range of different trading options and we are confident that she can continue to play an important operational role elsewhere in the world.' This came some weeks after St Helena Line was successful in winning a new contract to continue providing modified freight services by sea using a container ship.

As the official completion date of St Helena's airport approached, RMS *St Helena* started making special journeys by way of farewells, the first of which was to Tristan da Cunha. Thereafter she voyaged to the UK. The ship was given a tumultuous welcome as she passed through London's Tower Bridge to berth in the Pool of London alongside HMS *Belfast*. At this time, it was anticipated that *St Helena* would retire from her historic service later in the year.

An open day gave opportunity for enthusiasts and 'Saints' in the UK to visit the ship. HRH The Princess Royal attended a reception aboard, having previously travelled on the 'RMS' between St Helena and Ascension in 2002.

After a visit to the Port of London Cruise Terminal at Tilbury, and subsequent loading at the cargo facility, *St Helena* set her sights once again for her distant home. Due to problems with St Helena's airport, a decision was made to extend the operation of the ship until

July 2017. This was to help mitigate fears felt by tourism companies on the island whose businesses would have been threatened by a lack of tourists able to reach St Helena.

The affection in which RMS *St Helena* is held by the 'Saints' manifests itself in many ways, brought to focus by the reality of the airport and the consequent eventual withdrawal of the ship. In 2015, the island's Arts and Crafts Association honoured the ship by making a presentation at St Helena Museum to her current two serving masters, made in thanks for the support the ship has given to the charities of the island over the years. The gift was a print of a painting commissioned to mark the end of the RMS era. It depicts the current ship, the previous RMS and a third vessel, *Southampton Castle,* which served the island as part of Union-Castle Line.

The community enthusiasm to try to retain *St Helena's* unique place in the island's heritage was charmingly manifest in the wish by some to preserve her as a floating hotel. Such undertakings are often both a minefield and a bottomless pit for financing. A more achievable aim is an RMS-themed décor of the Jamestown Hotel, portrayed by a planner enjoining us to 'Imagine enjoying – or frantically avoiding – beef tea on land at the Captain's table. That's the new vision for the hotel.' Staff will wear RMS-inspired uniforms, and memorabilia from the ship is to be strategically placed about the premises.

What makes the journey on RMS *St Helena* so special is the staff, meeting new people and a unique destination. The 'RMS experience' is a significant part of the St Helena experience. It encapsulates the golden era of sea travel.

When RMS *St Helena* eventually makes her final departure from St Helena, she will leave behind returned workers, age-old homecomings, the echoes of an era, boatmen, birdsong and the endless tolling of waves on the rocky shore.

***

Bibliography

atlantic-cable.com, *History of the Atlantic Cable & Submarine Telegraphy – 1899 – Cape Town –* St Helena Cable (2013).

Barrie, D., *Sextant* (William Collins, 2014).

Brooke, T., *A History of the Island of St Helena* (1808).

Darwin, C., *The Voyage of the Beagle* (Wordsworth Editions, 1997).

Gosse, P., *St Helena 1502–1938* (Anthony Nelson, 1990).

Hearl, T. W., *St Helena Britannica* (Society of Friends of St Helena, 2013).

H. M. Yacht Britannia: Voyage Round the World 1956–1957 Private Edition 337.

Kauffmann. J-P., *The Dark Room at Longwood* (Harvill Press, 1999).

Livermore, H., *Santa Helena, A Forgotten Portuguese Discovery* (2004).

Madden, R., *St Helena: A Green and Pleasant Alcatraz* (Telegraph, 1999).

Miller, W. H., *Union-Castle Liners* (Amberley Publishing, 2013).

Mitchell, W. H., *The Cape Run: The Story of the Union-Castle Service to South Africa and of the Ships Employed* (Terence Dalton, 1984).

Montgomerie, B., *The First 'St Helena': The East India Company Schooner St Helena, 1814–1830* (Printsetters, 1994).

Morriss, R., *Napoleon & St Helena 1815–1816* (University of Exeter Press, 1997).

Nathan, A. J., 'Boer Prisoners of War on the Island of St Helena', *Military History Journal,* 11 No. 3/4 (October 1999).

Newspapers: *St Helena Herald; St Helena Sentinel.*

Slocum, J., *Sailing Alone Around the World* (Sheridan House, 1981).

Smallman, D., *Quincentenary: A Story of St Helena, 1502–2002* (Patten Press, 2003).

Sobel, D., *Longitude* (London Fourth Estate, 1998).

Steiner, S., *St Helena* (Bradt, 2007).

Verdon, F., *The Other Way Around: Memoir of a Sea Journey Around the World* (Radcliffe Press, 1996).

Wilson, R. A., *RMS St Helena and the South Atlantic Islands* (Whittles Publishing, 2006).

Winchester, S., *Atlantic* (Harper Press, 2010).

Woodfield Captain, T., *Polar Mariner* (Whittles Publishing, 2016).